Life Through God's Word

Life Through God's Word

PSALM 119

Christopher J. H. Wright

PREACHING RESOURCES

© 2020 Christopher J. H. Wright

Published 2020 by Langham Preaching Resources
An imprint of Langham Publishing
www.langhampublishing.org

Langham Publishing and its imprints are a ministry of Langham Partnership

Langham Partnership
PO Box 296, Carlisle, Cumbria, CA3 9WZ, UK
www.langham.org

ISBNs:
978-1-78368-890-6 Print
978-1-83973-049-8 ePub
978-1-83973-050-4 Mobi
978-1-83973-051-1 PDF

First published by Authentic Media (2006) ISBN: 978-1-85078-6-948

Christopher J. H. Wright has asserted his right under the Copyright, Designs and Patents Act, 1988 to be identified as the Author of this work.

All rights reserved. No part of this publication may be reproduced, stored in a retrieval system or transmitted, in any form or by any means, electronic, mechanical, photocopying, recording or otherwise, without the prior written permission of the publisher or the Copyright Licensing Agency.

Requests to reuse content from Langham Publishing are processed through PLSclear. Please visit www.plsclear.com to complete your request.

Scriptures taken from the Holy Bible, New International Version®, NIV®. Copyright © 1973, 1978, 1984, 2011 by Biblica, Inc.™ Used by permission of Zondervan.

British Library Cataloguing-in-Publication Data
A catalogue record for this book is available from the British Library

ISBN: 978-1-78368-890-6

Cover & Book Design: projectluz.com

Langham Partnership actively supports theological dialogue and an author's right to publish but does not necessarily endorse the views and opinions set forth here or in works referenced within this publication, nor can we guarantee technical and grammatical correctness. Langham Partnership does not accept any responsibility or liability to persons or property as a consequence of the reading, use or interpretation of its published content.

To
the Chad branch
of the Summer Institute of Linguistics (SIL)

Contents

Preface..ix
Using This Book 1
Introduction to Psalm 119... 3

Section 1
   Personal Commitment and the Word of Truth (Psalm 119:57–64) 7
1. God's Word as the Focus of Faith and Commitment 11
   (Psalm 119:89–96, 137–144, 151, 160)
2. God's Word as the Focus of Love and Obedience 19
   (Psalm 119:14–16, 20, 24, 34–36, 44–48, 72, 92–97, 103,
     111–112, 127–131, 163–167)

Section 2
   Personal Guidance and the Word of Light (Psalm 119:97–105) 29
3. Light for the Path 33
   (Psalm 119:1–9, 101–105)
4. Learning for the Pupil 43
   (Psalm 119:26–27, 33–34, 97–104)

Section 3
   Personal Sin and the Word of Grace (Psalm 119:9–16)................51
5. Awareness of Sin.. 55
   (Psalm 119:129–136)
6. Avoiding Sin: Strengthening Our Minds and Wills................ 61
   (Psalm 119:9–16)
7. Avoiding Sin: Strengthening Our Emotions and Faith............. 69
   (Psalm 119:73–80, 153–160)

Section 4
   Personal Struggle and the Word of Lament (Psalm 119:81–88) 75

8 When Life Gets Tough. 79
   (Psalm 119:19–25, 81–88, 141–147)

9 How Does It Feel?. 85
   (Psalm 119:25–28, 81–83, 113–120)

10 Pressing On. 93
   (Psalm 119:145–160)

Section 5
   Personal Renewal and the Word of Life (Psalm 119:153–160). 101

11 Threats to Life. 105
   (Psalm 119:25–40)

12 Sources of Life. 113
   (Psalm 119:169–176)

   Conclusion 127

Preface

It was a surprise and a privilege when Jonathan Lamb, then chairman of the Keswick Council, invited me to give morning Bible readings at Keswick in July 1998. I accepted gladly. My enthusiasm dimmed somewhat when Jonathan later wrote to say that the Council wondered if I would like to consider a series of five expositions of Psalm 119. That was more of a challenge, and it was some time before I agreed that it was a challenge well worth tackling.

But how to go about it? I have heard from a good friend who led a study of Psalm 119 with a group of about twenty men. Each week, he asked them to memorize one of the twenty-two eight-verse sections of the psalm and then to produce their own poem that expressed their own faith and struggles. When they met, each of them would recite their poem and the relevant verses of the psalm before the group began to discuss and pray around that section of the psalm. But I was only going to speak five times at Keswick, not twenty-two times, and several thousand personal poems from all those attending would have been difficult to handle. So a different approach was needed.

I also knew that I could not simply teach the longest psalm in the Bible verse by verse over five days. So I read it and reread it, at home, on train journeys, all over the place, until eventually several key themes began to crystallize in my mind. These then took shape as five Bible studies, which have now become the five main sections of this book.

I am glad to have the opportunity to put the material into this format for personal or group Bible study and for use by preachers. I am thankful to Jonathan Lamb for the original invitation and to Keswick Ministries and Authentic for seeing it through to publication, and to Lucy Atherton for her editing of the first edition. Likewise, I am grateful to Isobel Stevenson and Morag Venter for the work involved in editing it for this second edition.

The final section, "Personal Renewal and the Word of Life," was written in Africa in the company of a fine group of people – the fifty or so members of the Chad branch of the Summer Institute of Linguistics (SIL). It was a time of great encouragement and blessing as I listened to them talk about their work of translating the Bible into some of the many languages spoken in Chad that do not yet have the Bible in written form. Their commitment to the truth, relevance and life-giving power of God's word reminded me again and again of Psalm 119. They were enduring some of the same struggles, stresses and suffering that the writer of this psalm endured. So this book is dedicated to them, with admiration for their labours, praise to God for what he is accomplishing through them, and gratitude for a week of blessing spent in their company.

Chris Wright
May 2020

Using This Book

The aim of this study guide is to help bridge the gap between the Bible world and our own. Chris Wright's exposition of Psalm 119 has vibrant meaning for us as believers in the 21st century. The questions that follow will help you to relate the principles he draws out to your own lives and situations. You can use this guide either for your own devotional time with God or as part of a group. Enjoy your study!

Using This Book for Personal Study

Begin by praying and reading through the passage and commentary a number of times before looking at the questions. You may find it helpful to note down your answers to the questions and any other thoughts you may have. Putting pen to paper will help you think through the issues and how they specifically apply to your own situation. It will also be encouraging to look back over all that God has been teaching you!

Talk about what you're learning with a friend. Pray together that you'll be able to apply all these new lessons to your life.

Using This Book in Small Groups: A Note to Group Leaders

In preparation for the study, pray and then read the passage of Scripture and the associated commentary a number of times. Use other resource material such as a Bible dictionary or atlas if they would be helpful. Each week think through what materials you need for the study – a flip chart, pens and paper, other Bible translations, worship music?

At the top of each chapter we have stated the aim – this is the heart of the passage and the truth you want your group to take away with them. With this in mind, decide which questions and activities you should spend most time on. Add questions that would be helpful to your group or particular church situation.

Before people come, encourage them to read the passage and commentary that you will be studying that week.

Make sure you leave time at the end of the study for the "Reflect and Respond" section so that the group members are able to apply what they are learning to their own situation.

Preaching from Psalm 119

Just a note for preachers. This title is published by Langham Preaching Resources, and there are Langham Preaching movements now established in many parts of the world. We encourage preachers to focus on three issues, and my hope is that these points are in some sense modelled in this study guide.

- *Am I being faithful* to the Bible passage: am I reflecting the meaning of the passage, so that I truly express what the original writer intended his original hearers to understand?
- *Am I being clear*: is the way I present the message structured in a way that helps the listener or reader truly understand the force and flow of the passage?
- *Am I being relevant*: am I making the connections with the lives of my hearers, demonstrating how the Bible passage applies to the challenges of their personal, family, and church lives, as well as the mood and worldview of their culture?

These are three good questions for anyone seeking to explain a Bible passage, whether in preaching, in small groups, or in one-to-one explanation of the passage to others.

Introduction to Psalm 119

It is said that in the 1740s an English minister named William Grimshaw would leave his congregation reciting a psalm while he went out to chase reluctant parishioners into church. If there were many absentees and he assumed the task would take some time, he would tell the congregation to recite Psalm 119.

Everybody knows that Psalm 119 is the longest psalm in the book of Psalms. And even those who only glance at it rapidly can see that it refers to God's word or God's law in almost every single verse. Some people find this repetitive and boring, and don't bother to dig deeper, which is a pity for Psalm 119 is actually a superbly written poem.

Unfortunately, it is difficult to see an important aspect of this poem when we read it in translation. It was composed as an acrostic, a literary form in which each line of a poem begins with the next letter in the alphabet. So the first line would begin with *a*, the next with *b*, and the third with *c*, and so on. The same technique is used in Psalms 111 and 112, a matched pair of psalms in which the first deals with the righteousness of God, while the second deals with the righteousness of the person who fears God.

But the author of Psalm 119 was not content to use a single line per letter. He had so much to say that he needed eight lines per letter! So he composed a vast tapestry of a psalm, with 22 stanzas (one for each letter of the Hebrew alphabet) with each stanza being eight lines long. That is why many English Bibles have the name or symbol for a Hebrew letter at the start of each block of verses in Psalm 119.

Then, to enrich his work still more, the poet found eight different ways of referring to the word of God. Some of the words are very similar in meaning, but there are subtle differences between them. Here they are in the order they are introduced to us in the psalm. (The translation given in italics is the one normally used in the NIV.)

These words are all woven together, like the threads of a tapestry, giving texture and colour. Or to use a musical metaphor, we could say that they provide the constant background rhythm of the poem.

Verse	Hebrew word	Approximate meaning
1	*Torah*	*The law* as a whole; basically meaning guidance
2	*'edoth*	*Statutes*, testimonies, witness
4	*Piqqudim*	*Precepts*, detailed instructions
5	*Huqqim*	*Decrees*, inscribed and binding
6	*Miswoth*	*Commands*, orders
7	*Mispatim*	*Laws*, judgments, decisions, precedents
9	*Dabar*	*Word*
38	*'imrah*	*Promise*

Looking at these words, some might be tempted to say that this is a "psalm in honour of the Law" – a kind of dry and dusty sermon encouraging subservience or, even worse, legalism. But in fact, the psalm is not really about the law directly at all. Apart from the first three verses, the whole poem is *entirely addressed to God*. The most repeated words in the psalm are not words for the law but "you" and "your." In other words, this psalm is all about a relationship. It is an extended prayer, a testimony, a plea, a complaint, a reassurance, that comes out of deep personal experience and an intimate relationship with God. That's what we should discover as we study it carefully together.

So what benefit will there be for us in soaking ourselves in Psalm 119 for however long it takes to work through this book? I think we will find that it mirrors for us what is probably the common experience of so many believers. Here is someone who not only speaks to us but speaks for us.

What kind of person can we see behind this poetic work of art? I believe we see

- a person with a strong love for God and for God's word.
- a person with a deep desire to live in a way that pleases God.
- a person who knows that this will bring joy, blessing, freedom and fullness of life.
- a person who wants to walk in the right way and avoid doing what is wrong and sinful, but needs help to do so.
- a person who is going through experiences of real stress, difficulty, external threat and internal fear, exhaustion, failure and vulnerability, and who is showing signs of depression.
- a person who longs for God to meet those needs and to renew, protect and sustain their life.
- a person who knows that God is loving, gracious, righteous and merciful and who knows all this from the Scriptures.

If some or all of those things find an echo in your heart, then here is a good travelling companion for your journey. And if you are planning to preach from this Psalm, it is very likely that there will be people in your congregation for whom some of those things are part of their experience too.

Rather than trying to work through the psalm verse by verse, it seemed better to identify some of the major themes that recur again and again and to look at those in depth. So you will find that each section of this book begins with a recommendation that you read a portion of the psalm that focuses on the theme we will be studying in that section of the book. Those studying the psalm as part of a group may find it helpful to read these verses aloud. Here in advance are the topics we shall consider. Each one is a pair, putting together the psalmist's own emotions and needs and the dimension of God's word that spoke to those emotions and needs.

Section	Topic	Recommended portion (verses)
1	Personal Commitment and the Word of Truth	57–64
2	Personal Guidance and the Word of Light	97–105
3	Personal Sin and the Word of Grace	9–16
4	Personal Struggle and the Word of Lament	81–88
5	Personal Renewal and the Word of Life	153–160

Before we start on the study, I suggest that you find time to read through the whole psalm, slowly and appreciatively. Try to savour its moods and emotions, and pray the psalmist's prayer with him.

Section 1

Personal Commitment and the Word of Truth

Psalm 119:57–64

Personal Commitment and the Word of Truth

Introduction to Section 1

I have long been involved in the world of cross-cultural mission, partly through working in India for five years, but much more through the thirteen years that I worked at All Nations Christian College before joining the Langham Partnership. While at All Nations and when visiting many former students in their places of service, I have been amazed at and humbled by the depth of commitment shown by men and women in mission, a commitment that flows from their deepest values and convictions.

- I have marvelled at medical and paramedical workers exposing themselves to the horrors and dangers of Afghanistan in its worst times because they are convinced that every human being – of whatever faith, with all their limbs or none – matters personally to God and is to be loved and served for his sake. One former student returned from there and spoke at All Nations. At the end of his talk, he casually took some spent bullets from his pocket and said he would give them to anybody wanting to pray for him. He had dug them out of the walls of his bedroom, his lampshade and his door while living in the war zone.
- I read the words of a midwife in the deserts of North Africa, struggling with her own appalling back pain, talking of the infinite worth of every tiny baby she delivers and the deep grief she shares with any mother at losing a child of God.
- I have seen Christian conservationists handling tiny birds with tender affection, convinced that all creation has value. If no sparrow falls to earth without our heavenly Father knowing it, then sparrows are worthy of our care too.
- I listened as a woman serving in Chad told me of her struggle with chronic exhaustion syndrome and other debilitating illnesses while continuing to translate portions of Scripture into a local language. "It is the word of God, after all," she said. "They need it. God gave me the skills to give it to them. What else can I do?"

Such stories could be multiplied. They are stories of deep commitment, and in all cases that commitment flows out of the person's core beliefs.

It is obvious that the person who wrote Psalm 119 is totally *committed* – heart, soul, body, mind and spirit – to God, to God's word and to God's ways. And the reason for this passionate commitment is not hard to discover. It is because his whole *worldview* is shaped by the conviction that God's word is true and trustworthy. The poet's whole life is built upon this core belief, even though at times that life could be tough and uncomfortable. *Commitment* to God's word grows out of *convictions* about God's word.

So let us look, then, at some of the ways this psalmist explained these convictions about God's word (which in this psalm is most often referred to as "God's law"). We will find that God's word is the focus of the psalmist's belief, trust, love, delight and obedient commitment. Here is someone who is responding to God's word intellectually, emotionally and behaviourally. Head, heart and hands are all engaged.

1

God's Word as the Focus of Faith and Commitment

AIM: To focus on the transcendent qualities of God's word

Focus on the Theme

What are the things you care most about in life? Morals, justice, equality, evangelism? In what ways does the Bible shape your core beliefs and commitments? A key statement to start us off is the simple affirmation of verse 66 that "I trust your commands."

Read: Psalm 119:89–96, 137–144, 151, 160

Key verse: Psalm 119:66

Outline

1. God's word is eternal and universal (vv. 89–91, 96)
2. God's word is righteous and moral (vv. 128, 137–138, 172)
3. God's word is true and real (vv. 142, 151, 160)

Conclusion

When the psalmist says, "I trust your commands" (v. 66) he means that he has complete confidence in them. This involves far more than mere blind obedience to a code of rules. What he means is, "I understand these words, I agree with them, I am committed to their truth and validity, I lean on them, I know I can depend on them." He is exercising intelligent faith in the trustworthiness of the commands of God when he declares, "All your commands are trustworthy" (v. 86).

Why does the psalmist have such intellectual and moral confidence in God's word? The answer is embedded in a chain of verses throughout the psalm in which he expresses his conviction that the word of God is *eternal*, *righteous* and *true*. Let's look at each of these qualities in turn.

1. God's Word Is Eternal and Universal (vv. 89–91, 96)

God's word must share in God's eternal, transcendent nature. If there is only one, true, living God who owns, rules and fills the whole universe, then the word of that God must likewise be universal. And this is what the psalmist states. Read the following verses and consider their vast implications.

> Your word, LORD, is eternal;
>   it stands firm in the heavens.
> Your faithfulness continues through all generations;
>   you established the earth, and it endures.
> Your laws endure to this day,
>   for all things serve you. (vv. 89–91)

> To all perfection I see a limit;
>   but your commands are boundless. (v. 96)

> Long ago I learned from your statutes
>   that you established them to last forever. (v. 152)

We should not think that these verses mean God's laws are somehow timeless in the sense of being abstract principles unrelated to any particular local context. On the contrary, all God's words were given within a specific history and culture, and that is why they had such sharp relevance at the time. However, through that original specific grounding, these words of God have an enduring quality that continues to speak authoritatively and relevantly. So we can read words that God spoke through Moses at Mount Sinai more than a thousand years before Christ. We can read words he spoke in Jerusalem through Isaiah and Jeremiah, seven or eight centuries before Christ. We can read words written by Paul to new believers in Corinth a few decades after Christ. And we can still hear God speaking right into our hearts today, when we learn how to listen properly. That is what the psalmist is observing. So, even though he probably lived centuries after the original giving of the law, he affirms its abiding and universal relevance.

Another psalmist said that God's law was "more precious than gold" and "sweeter than honey" (Ps 19:10). The writer of Psalm 119 might have changed the phrase "diamonds are forever" to "God's word is forever."

- Even the best that humans can achieve is limited. By contrast, what do these verses say about God's commands? How do they set God's law in a universal framework?

- Think about the difference between the local contexts in which God's commands were given, and their relevance for all times and places. Why do you think God gave his law? What was his intention?

- How do we respond to God's commands today?

---

2. God's Word Is Righteous and Moral (vv. 128, 137–138, 172)

The law not only shares God's eternal and universal nature, it also reflects God's moral character, his righteousness, justice, integrity and compassion. And it does so fully, objectively and purposefully. Read the following groups of verses and reflect on what they state and on the psalmist's response.

> You are righteous, LORD,
>   and your laws are right.
> The statutes you have laid down are righteous;
>   they are fully trustworthy. (vv. 137–138)
>
> and because I consider all your precepts right,
>   I hate every wrong path. (v. 128)
>
> Your statutes are always righteous;
>   give me understanding that I may live. (v. 144)
>
> May my tongue sing of your word,
>   for all your commands are righteous. (v. 172)

The Hebrew words translated "righteous" and "righteousness" refer to something that is truly what it is supposed to be, to something that sets the standard or norm by which everything else can be measured. In the context of this psalm, it is God's word and God's law that provides the standard by which our behaviour is measured. They are the straight edge or the plumb line. This is where we bring all our ethical or moral opinions and choices for testing.

So it is because God's law is righteous that it is trustworthy (think of accurate weights and measures) and it is because God himself is righteous that his word shares the same moral quality.

- What is the link between being right and being trustworthy? How does this affect our everyday lives (for example, clocks, scales)? How does this affect our trust in God's moral teaching in Scripture?
- What is the psalmist's personal response to his knowledge that God's law is morally perfect?
- How can we imitate the psalmist's responses in our lives in relation to God's word? Think about the balance he has between moral effort (v. 128) and hearty singing (v. 172).
- Think back over the last year. When has a passage of Scripture been like a "straight edge" in your life, setting a standard of righteousness for your attitude or behaviour in some situation? Is there a passage of Scripture that is doing this right now?

---

3. God's Word Is True and Real (vv. 142, 151, 160)

> Your righteousness is everlasting
>   and your law is true. (v. 142)

> Yet you are near, LORD,
>   and all your commands are true. (v. 151)

> All your words are true;
>   all your righteous laws are eternal. (v. 160)

Verse 160 literally says "the sum, or the totality, of your words is true." Here the psalmist is not so much thinking of every individual word as true; rather, he is saying that God's full revelation of himself in the words of Scripture constitutes the truth, and so can be trusted forever.

We can define "truth" as what matches reality. It is the faithful reflection of what is actually the case. This means that a statement can only be true (or false) if it refers to something that is real. For example, the statement "sea water is salty" is true because the sea exists and humans have long used it as a source of salt. But the statement that "fairies have wings" is neither true nor false because there are no fairies (except in children's stories).

When we say that "the word of God is true" we mean that it refers to reality – the ultimate reality of God and his ability to communicate. We also mean that everything that God's word teaches is part of reality. His word reveals the reality of the creation, the reality of our human life in the image of God, the reality of our sin and brokenness, the reality of God's action in history for the redemption of humanity and all creation. These things are real. This is the way it really is. This is how we came to be where we are, and this is how God intends to take things to where he plans.

So when this psalmist makes these great claims for the word of God, he is speaking about a lot more than just its factual accuracy. He means that God's word is where he finds a truthful, dependable account of what is "really real." And that is what he builds all his life and hope upon. Anything else is sinking sand.

- The verses quoted in this section use three of the eight different words used for God's law in Psalm 119[1] and make the same statement about each of them: They are true. Check this for yourself.

- Read the verses that precede each of the quoted sections. What do they show about the circumstances of the psalmist?

- How should our confidence in the truth of God's word sustain us in difficult times? Can you give examples of when it has done so for you?

Conclusion

Putting our three points together then, our Psalmist looks at the word of God, and makes it the object of his total trust. That is to say, he sees it as a solid, objective, dependable reality.

---

[1]. See Introduction, page 4.

- It is universal in its scope and relevance.
- It is normative, providing moral standards and making moral demands.
- It is reliable in its truth claims.

Now these are vast claims. And they are controversial claims too – at least in the West. Many now believe that there is no transcendent, eternal reality, no objective universal morality, and no absolute or final truth. They regard the search for such certainties through religion, or philosophy, or even through science as misguided, pointless and oppressive. They insist that no culture, no religion, no ideology (including the ideology of science) embodies universally valid truth. All is relative. Everything ebbs and flows in the great tides of history and culture. Life is like a carnival, so enjoy the variety as it passes by, but don't look for depth or ultimate foundations. There are none. There is no ultimate reality – only image. There is no ultimate morality – only what is good for you. There is no ultimate eternity – only the surface experience of the present.

What does Psalm 119 have to say in response to such thinking? The affirmation of this psalm is that:

- There is an eternal transcendent reality – the living, personal Creator and Redeemer God, to whom we have access through his word.
- There is a universally relevant moral standard that applies to all human beings in every age and culture. We have access to it through God's word, though he has planted an awareness of it in all who are made in his own image (see Rom 1:19–20).
- There is an objective truth – an account, an explanation, a worldview that faithfully corresponds to the way things really are, and we have access to as much of it as we can grasp.

Our acceptance of this worldview, like all human knowing, is based on faith – reasonable, warranted faith. You can stand on and defend this faith; it is one upon which you can build your life, choices and future.

That is where this psalmist stands. God's word is the focus of his faith. Is that where we stand too?

Further Study

Read Leviticus 5:14–19; 25:8–31; Numbers 14:3–21 and 1 Corinthians 11:4–10.

How do we go about finding the relevance and authority of passages of the Bible that were not originally written to us? How do we move from their specific context, through the wider intention of God as embodied in them, to our own specific circumstances? How do we apply such passages in our own contexts? Try and list some examples of how that works.

Reflection and Response

Jesus is God's living word (see John 1), and he claimed to be "the way and the truth and the life" (John 14:6).

- What aspects of the word of God, highlighted in the study above, are filled out and made personal in Jesus?

- How does that affect the way we combine our Bible reading with our relationship with Christ and our obedience to him?

Regular preaching of the Bible is one way that we can strengthen people's trust in the truth of God's word and their commitment to believing and obeying it. If you are a preacher, is this your conscious aim? And how could you work towards it by preaching from this psalm?

2

God's Word as the Focus of Love and Obedience

> **AIM: To examine the strength of our emotional and obedient response to God's word**

Focus on the Theme

The psalmist revels in God's word. He uses all kinds of colourful, warm and emotional language about it, and he does this most often when he is talking about God's law. This may come as a shock to those who thought that the Old Testament was all about legalism and cold obedience to external codes. In this chapter we will see how God's law is a joy and a delight, an object of love and very precious.

Read: Psalm 119:14–16, 20, 24, 34–36, 44–48, 72, 92–97, 103, 111–112, 127–131, 163–167

Key verse: Psalm 119:97

Outline

1. God's law is a joy and delight (vv. 14–16, 24, 35, 47, 70, 92, 142, 162, 174)
2. God's law is loved (48, 54–55, 61–62, 93, 97, 109, 113, 131, 140, 163–167, 176)
3. God's law is precious (vv. 32, 45, 72, 103, 127)

> 4. God's law requires obedience (119:66)
>   a. With all my heart (vv. 2, 10, 30, 34, 36, 58, 112, 145)
>   b. Fully, forever and now (vv. 5, 20, 44)

1. God's Law Is a Joy and Delight (vv. 14–16, 24, 35, 47, 70, 92, 142, 162, 174)

We tend to use words like "joy," "enjoy," "enjoyable" and "rejoicing" in contexts where we are happy in the company of those we love, or when we receive something we have longed for, or when enjoying the beauty of nature. But the psalmist uses these words in a context that may surprise us:

> I rejoice in following your statutes
> as one rejoices in great riches. (v. 14)
>
> I rejoice in your promise
> like one who finds great spoil. (v. 162)

This tells us something about his attitude to God's law. Not only does it give him joy, he also finds it a source of delight. Look at these verses:

> I delight in your decrees;
> I will not neglect your word. (v. 16)
>
> Your statutes are my delight;
> they are my counsellors. (v. 24)
>
> Direct me in the paths of your commands,
> for there I find delight. (v. 35)
>
> For I delight in your commands
> because I love them. (v. 47)

It is worth noting that he doesn't just say this because everything is going so well for him that he is feeling good about the world in general. In fact, the exact opposite is true, as we can see from the following verses:

> Their hearts are callous and unfeeling,
> but I delight in your law. (v. 70)
>
> If your law had not been my delight,
> I would have perished in my affliction. (v. 92)

> Trouble and distress have come upon me,
>> but your commands give me delight. (v. 143)
>
> I long for your salvation, LORD,
>> and your law gives me delight. (v. 174)

- What gives you joy and delight? Does it include God's word and his commands? If so, what does this mean in practical terms?
- Read the verses surrounding the "delight" (verses 70, 92, 143, and 174). What do they tell about the realities of the psalmist's life? Do they throw light on why he finds delight in God's law?
- Can you testify to a time when verse 143 was true for you?

---

2. God's Law Is Loved (vv. 48, 54–55, 61–62, 93, 97, 109, 113, 131, 140, 163–167, 176)

While we may use the language of delight on a regular basis, we are rather more careful about who or what we apply the word "love" to. The language of love is not at all out of place, however, when the psalmist thinks of God's law. In fact, the psalmist emphasizes it.

> I reach out for your commands, which I love. (v. 48)
>
> Oh how I love your law!
>> I meditate on it all day long. (v. 97)
>
> I hate double-minded people,
>> but I love your law. (v. 113)
>
> I open my mouth and pant,
>> longing for your commands. (v. 131)

The language is emotive and expressive, and even physical in its longing. (v. 131). The Hebrew verb used is the same one that is used for loving God, loving our neighbour, and loving a spouse.

If you truly love someone, you don't forget them, even when you are far away from home or in the middle of the night (vv. 54–55). A few summers ago, my wife spent two weeks in Canada for a family wedding. I was unable to go for work reasons. It was an unusual experience for her to be the one travelling and me to be the one left at home. But did we forget each other? Of course not. Last thing at night and first thing in the morning I put my head on her pillow and prayed for her (though I can't say that I rose at midnight to give her thanks, v. 62!). So when the psalmist keeps on saying he will never forget God's law, it shows just how much he loves God's law.

The psalmist would not forget God's words even in the face of opposition (v. 61) or danger (v. 109). He knew that they had saved him in the past (v. 93) and he trusted that they would help him find his way in the present and in the future (v. 176).

- How should loving God's word affect our attitude to it? Can we identify with what the psalmist says in verse 131?

- What particular benefit of loving God's law is mentioned in verse 165? How different is this from the seeing his laws as a burden and a straightjacket?

- What tends to make us forget God's word? And what happens when we do?

---

3. God's Law Is Precious (vv. 32, 45, 72, 103, 127)

What is the most valuable thing you can think of? Gold? Silver? God's law is more precious than either. It is so valuable, so precious to the psalmist, that it can only be described in superlatives.

> The law from your mouth is more precious to me
> > than thousands of pieces of silver and gold. (v. 72)
>
> I love your commands
> > more than gold, more than pure gold. (v. 127)

What is the sweetest thing you can think of? Honey? God's word tastes even better.

> How sweet are your words to my taste,
> > sweeter than honey to my mouth! (v. 103)

Nothing is of more value than faithful obedience to God. Nothing is more satisfying than living according to his word. God's word, then, is not just the focus of intellectual assent and faith. It is also the focus of our emotional delight, love and appreciation.

So, where is all this so-called Old Testament legalism referred to in the opening paragraph of this chapter? Where is all this bondage to the law? It is tragic that even as Christians we have been influenced by the cultural prejudice (which is actually as old as the fall of humanity in the garden of Eden) that obedience is somehow negative, implying loss of freedom. On the contrary, this psalmist revels in the fact that God's law was designed to improve human life and well-being. Obedience to God's law is the perfect recipe for true freedom, whether life is portrayed as running along a path or walking around in open spaces.

> I run in the path of your commands,
>   for you have broadened my understanding. (v. 32)

> I will walk about in freedom,
>   for I have sought out your precepts. (v. 45)

- How does the psalmist's claim to hold God's law in the number one position challenge the subconscious priorities that govern our everyday lives?

---

4. God's Law Requires Obedience (vv. 2, 5, 10, 20, 30, 34–36, 44, 58, 112, 145)

God's word (especially his "law") speaks to our minds; the psalmist *believes it* (v. 66 – see chapter 1). God's word also speaks to our emotions; the psalmist *loves* it. But God's word goes further than both the mind and the emotions. It also affects our will. We must choose to *obey it*.

Think of what Jesus said in John 14:15: "If you love me, keep my commands." The psalmist had heard something similar, for the book of Deuteronomy speaks of love for God and obedience to his law in virtually the same breath (Deut 6:4–9; 30:2, 6, 10). So the psalmist determines to put God's law into practice as a matter of constant, deliberate, willing choice. He intends to allow it to shape his thinking and living, or in other words, his head, heart and hands.

a. "With all my heart" (vv. 2, 10, 30, 34, 36, 58, 112, 145)

The psalmist uses the expression "with all my heart" about eight times, stressing his total personal commitment to obeying God's law. This, after all, was how Deuteronomy had summarized the primary responsibility of all Israelites, in the great affirmation and exhortation of the *Shema'*.

> Hear O Israel: The LORD our God, the LORD is one. Love the LORD your God with all your heart and with all your soul and with all your strength. (Deut 6:4–5)

Why did we not include this point in our last section about love, the more emotional response to God and his word? Surely "love with all your heart" is emotional language? Well, not entirely. The "heart" in Hebrew was not so much the seat of your emotions as the seat of your will. Emotions tended to be located lower down the body (in the bowels, for example) where you felt pity, compassion, tenderness. The heart, for an Israelite, was where you did your thinking. The heart was where you made your decisions and choices. The heart was what governed your intentions and planning. The heart, in other words, was the source of your actual behaviour – good and bad. That is why Jesus could say, "it is from within, out of a person's heart that evil thoughts come – sexual immorality, theft, murder, adultery, greed, malice, deceit, lewdness, envy, slander, arrogance and folly" (Mark 7:21–22). In this he echoed the original verdict on the human heart in Genesis 6:5. You need to watch your heart if you want to change your behaviour.

This psalmist wanted the law of God to govern his heart, so he put his whole heart into it:

> Blessed are those who keep his statutes
>   and seek him with all their heart. (v. 2)

> I seek you with all my heart;
>   do not let me stray from your commands. (v. 10)

> I have chosen the way of faithfulness;
>   I have set my heart on your laws. (v. 30)

> Give me understanding, so that I may keep your law
>   and obey it with all my heart. (v. 34)

> Turn my heart towards your statutes
>   and not towards selfish gain. (v. 36)

> I have sought your face with all my heart;
> > be gracious to me according to your promise. (v. 58)
>
> My heart is set on keeping your decrees
> > to the very end. (v. 112)
>
> I call with all my heart; answer me, LORD,
> > and I will obey your decrees. (v. 145)

- Read the "heartbeat" verses above and consider the different things that the psalmist says he will do with all his heart, the things his heart is set on. How does that apply to your own choices and actions?

b. "Fully, forever and now" (vv. 5, 20, 44)

Shallow obedience is one of the things that Jesus both warned against and complained about. This psalmist is determined that commitment to God and his word will be total and lasting, for he knows that there is no point in promising something "forever" if it doesn't include "today."

> Oh, that my ways were steadfast
> > in obeying your decrees! (v. 5)
>
> My soul is consumed with longing
> > for your laws at all times. (v. 20)
>
> I will always obey your law,
> > for ever and ever. (v. 44)

- What does the word "choice" mean in today's world? "Tea today, coffee tomorrow"? Choices can change with tastes or fashions. So what does the psalmist mean when he says, "I have chosen the way of faithfulness" in verse 30?

- What kind of commitments have you made, if any, that match the language of "at all times" and "for ever and ever"?

Further Study

Read Matthew 13:31–52.

What did Jesus say about our priorities? Think of his sayings about the kingdom of God as the supreme value, priority and "prize" in life, and about what matters most in life.

Reflection and Response

Think about the culture and characteristics of the particular Christian group that you belong to (your church, or denomination, or favourite Christian gathering or festival). Does it balance the three things we have studied above: solid teaching for the mind; healthy enthusiasm for the emotions, and clear moral guidelines for biblical obedience? If not, where does the imbalance lie and what could you do to correct it?

If you are a preacher, ask yourself if your regular preaching of the Bible aims at the same balance: to give people food for their minds, healthy emotions (which doesn't mean only happy ones!), and a challenge to obedience. What changes and plans should you make?

Conclusion to Section 1

The two studies in this section challenge us all to check our personal commitment to the word of God in our lives. I think it particularly speaks to those who are most affected by the culture of postmodernity, especially in the West. There is a lot about the postmodern shift that is welcome and friendly to the gospel. We may indeed welcome its greater emphasis on

- the narrative dimension of life (we all love stories, and live out our stories);
- the significance of the local and cultural context in which we live;
- the value of all cultures and the need to overcome our inborn prejudices;
- living in relation to others, rather than adopting an individualistic lifestyle;
- resistance to domination and oppression.

However, when postmodern culture denies *any* absolute foundations, *any* ultimate truth, *any* non-negotiable objective reality, *any* universally valid moral standards, we must challenge it. Can you build the foundations of your life on a swamp or a moving walkway?

Here in Psalm 119 we are in the company of someone who is

- intellectually convinced about the eternal transcendence, moral value and final truth of God's word.
- emotionally excited about God's word, finding it to be the object of delight, love and highest priorities; and
- whole-heartedly committed to obeying God's word in every part of life.

All three of the above must work together if we are to live with radical and balanced Christian discipleship and obedience.

If we focus only on our intellectual convictions about God's word, our faith will be dry and academic. We may be doctrinally sound, but we will lack life and warmth and our faith may not have any practical effects.

If we focus only on our emotional commitment to God's word, our faith risks being little more than frothy emotionalism and excitement, with no depth of understanding. We may slip into the hypocrisy of enthusiasm without genuine practical obedience.

If we are only committed to obeying God, without our minds and emotions being involved, we may explode into hasty and enthusiastic action without knowledge and without wisdom. The result may be disillusionment or legalism, when the love and joy are lost.

Being balanced Christians has to involve our minds, our emotions, and our wills. And, for those of us who are called to regular preaching ministry, that is also the balance that we should strive for in our preaching and in its impact on our people.

Section 2

Personal Guidance and the Word of Light

Psalm 119:97–105

Personal Guidance and the Word of Light

Introduction to Section 2

The old hymn "Onward Christian soldiers, marching as to war" is seldom sung these days.[1] Some of us prefer the different beat of "We are marching in the light of God."[2] Such songs make us think of a great army moving forward in step, in perfect formation (though armies can only do that on the parade ground, not in actual battle).

But the Bible seldom speaks of us marching. If anything, it speaks of *God* being on the march! Our own lives are more often described as walking purposefully along a path. For some of us, even that metaphor may not work. Our lives feel more like staggering unsteadily from one crisis to another, or wandering in increasing confusion through a maze of dead ends and blind choices.

We all long for clear guidance. Why else are horoscopes so popular? And as Christians we long to know "what God want us to do." We sometimes wish he would tell us clearly. Sometimes we think he has told us for certain, and then things don't turn out as we thought they should do if he really had. We would like to be wise and discerning in the choices we make. We really do want to do God's will and follow his plan for our lives.

So did this psalmist. He clearly wants to avoid sinning or making disastrous mistakes, but even more he wants God's help and protection during his struggle. He wants to live well in every sense of that word. He longs to be *wise* (intellectually), *godly* (spiritually) and *moral* (practically) in all the everyday things of life. And so he repeatedly asks God for two things:

- *Light for the path*, that is, guidance in making decisions.
- *Learning for the pupil*, that is, wisdom in his thinking.

These will be the topics for the two chapters in this section.

---

1. A processional hymn written in 1865 by Sabine Baring-Gould and sung to the music of Arthur Sullivan.

2. From the South African Zulu hymn *Siyahamba*, which was often used as a protest song during the apartheid years.

3

Light for the Path

> **AIM: To reconsider what the Bible means by "God's guidance in our lives"**

Focus on the Theme

The metaphor that life is a journey is often used in the Bible, and is still in everyday use in secular contexts too. How often have you heard someone refer to a career path or speaks about someone's way of life, meaning their behaviour, choices and actions? Or have you ever heard the comment that someone has "gone off the rails."

But if life is a journey, where is the map showing us the route? How do we know what choices and decisions to make at each fork in the road? Think of all the choices and decisions you made last year. Did you move house, apply for university, buy a car, go on a short-term mission trip? How did you make these decisions? What role did God play in your planning?

Read: Psalm 119:1–9, 101–105

Key verse: Psalm 119:1

Outline

1. Walking in the way of the Lord (1, 29, 30, 32, 59)
2. Watching your way with the word of God (vv. 9, 105)
   a. Guidance and the Bible
   b. Guidance or a blueprint (vv. 101, 104, 128)

In Christian circles, we used to sing a hymn that began

> When we walk with the Lord
> In the light of his word
> What a glory he sheds on our way![1]

Those lines echo the opening words of Psalm 119:

> Blessed are those whose ways are blameless,
>   who walk according to the law of the LORD. (v. 1)

1. Walking in the Way of the Lord (vv. 1, 29–30, 32, 59)

The psalmist saw life as a journey and frequently brought his way or ways before God as a matter of concern. We can get an impression of how he was thinking and of how he wanted to live from verses like these, in which the words "ways" and "path" come up repeatedly:

> Keep me from deceitful ways;
>   be gracious to me and teach me your law. (v. 29)

> I have chosen the way of faithfulness;
>   I have set my heart on your laws. (v. 30)

> I run in the path of your commands,
>   for you have broadened my understanding. (v. 32)

> I have considered my ways
>   and have turned my steps to your statutes. (v. 59)

The psalmist rejected "deceitful ways" and wanted to follow "the path of your commands." He is using a metaphor that can be traced all the way back to Genesis, where God reminded Abraham that he was not to follow the path of Sodom, but was to walk in a very different way:

> I have chosen him, so that he will direct his children and his household after him to keep the way of the LORD by doing what is right and just, so that the LORD will bring about for Abraham what he has promised him. (Gen 18:19)

---

1. These are the openings lines of the hymn known as "Trust and Obey," by John H. Sammis.

God's words make it clear that keeping in "the way of the Lord" involves "doing what is right and just." Righteousness and justice (two of the most important words in the ethical vocabulary of the Old Testament) were supposed to characterize the people descended from Abraham, namely the Israelites. Their mission was to walk in the way of the Lord, so that God could use them to bless the nations.

Centuries later, Moses uses the same metaphor when reminding the Israelites about God's requirements for them as his people:

> And now, Israel, what does the LORD your God ask of you but to *fear* the LORD your God, to *walk* in obedience to him, to *love* him, to *serve* the LORD your God with all your heart and with all your soul, and to *observe* the LORD's commands and decrees that I am giving you today for your own good? (Deut 10:12–13, italics added)

This verse is like a great chord of music, blending five distinct notes. What does God require? Only that we should *fear*, *walk*, *love*, *serve* and *obey* him. In other words, God is not just looking for obedience to the details of the surrounding laws in Deuteronomy, God is looking for lives that are fully committed to him.

But what does it mean to walk in the ways of the Lord? What are his ways that we should walk in them? The answer comes in the following verses:

> For the LORD your God is God of gods and Lord of lords, the great God, mighty and awesome, who shows no partiality and accepts no bribes. He defends the cause of the fatherless and the widow, and loves the foreigner residing among you, giving them food and clothing. And you are to love those who are foreigners, for you yourselves were foreigners in Egypt. (Deut 10:17–19)

The character of God is one of integrity, compassion, justice and practical care for those whom society has rejected. Therefore, to walk in his ways means to imitate these qualities in him.

Those that are careful to walk in this way can enjoy the promise of God's continued blessing. This is the same point made in the first verse of our psalm, as well as in the opening psalm of the whole book of Psalms.

> Blessed is the one
>   who does not walk in step with the wicked . . .
> For the LORD watches over the way of the righteous,
>   but the way of the wicked leads to destruction. (Ps 1:1, 6)

- Scan quickly through the rest of the psalm and find examples of other verses where the language of walking, running, feet, steps, a way or a path occurs. What does this tell us about the way the psalmist wanted to live? Can we say the same about ourselves?

2. Watching Your Way with the Word of God (vv. 9, 105)

It's all very well for God to watch the path of the righteous (Ps 1:6), but shouldn't we also watch our own path? If so, how can we do this? How am I to keep walking in the way of the Lord, when there are so many attractive alternatives and side-paths? That is a question the psalmist also asked, and answered:

> How can a young person stay on the path of purity?
>   By watching it according to your word. (v. 9, my paraphrase)

It is God's word that provides the light we need to know which path we should take. So we watch our footsteps with the help of God's word. It is light for the path. The psalmist goes on to say, in what has become a favourite verse for many, "Your word is a lamp for my feet, a light on my path" (v. 105).

- Think of a typical week, in work or at university, at home or wherever you may be. How can you work at "watching your way" in the light of God's word? How will this affect the things that you do?

a. Guidance and the Bible

Innumerable books offer us guidance on everything from how to live a successful Christian life to how to diet for Jesus (*What Would Jesus Eat?*) and how to train your dog the scriptural way. (I am serious! I have seen those books.) People aim to make plenty of money out of our anxieties.

But before you rush out to buy these *How to* books (with their ten easy steps to this or that spiritual achievement), remember that you already own the greatest resource in the matter of guidance. It's the Bible itself.

To say that is not to imply that the Bible is some sort of magic source of guidance, like a horoscope. We have all laughed at the story of what can happen when you randomly open a Bible and stick a pin on the page, hoping that the verse where the pin has landed is God's message to you: The first stab hits the following verse: "He [Judas] went away and hanged himself" (Matt 27:5). The second attempt stabs the following words: "Go and do likewise" (Luke 10:37)! Yet there are still many sincere Christians who seem to have a very similar approach when seeking God's guidance. For example, at All Nations Christian College there was a student who said that she was sure God had called her to mission in Latin America because she had prayed to God to guide her. Then, when she went into a shop that same day after her prayer, the first thing she saw was a big bag of Brazil nuts. A colleague wondered where she might have felt called to go if she had spotted the Mars bars!

No, the Bible is not a horoscope or a crystal ball. Nor is it enough just to have a Bible in our home or even in our hands and assume that we will be guided. But the Bible does offer guidance when used rightly on its own terms. That is, it provides guidance to those who have God's word stored in their hearts and on their lips, and who are committed to obeying. As Moses put it, "No, the word is very near you; it is in your mouth and in your heart so you may obey it" (Deut 30:14).

But even those who do love and seek to obey the Bible may not be wise in how they offer guidance from it. I can give you an example of this from my own family's experience. When we left Britain for India, we had some natural anxieties about the huge transition we were making and about moving to a strange land. In a prayer meeting shortly before our departure, a sincere brother "shared a word from God" with my wife. It was God's word to Jacob to overcome his fears about going to Egypt (which was obviously meant to represent India for us): "Do not be afraid to go down to Egypt, for I will . . . go down to Egypt with you, and I will surely bring you back again" (Gen 46:3–4). The brother assured Liz that God would go with us and God would bring us back. The brother meant well. I waited until later in the day before pointing out to Liz that the way God kept his promise to bring Jacob back from Egypt was to bring him home in a coffin. The verse was not quite as comforting as she had thought!

It seems that we need a better way to settle our anxieties in relation to God's guidance and providence. We need to study the whole of the Bible, and to have a grasp of sound principles of interpretation and application. This means that we need to get to know your Bible in depth and as a whole, so that it becomes part of our bloodstream. It should not only be the object of our study, but also the subject of our thinking. The Bible must not just be what we think *about*, but what we think *with*. Paul put it like this, "Let the message of Christ dwell among you richly" (Col 3:16).

In what ways does the Bible help us to discern God's guidance and keep walking in his ways? Here are some of the ways that occurred to me. Perhaps you can think of others.

- *The Bible gives us access to the mind and values of God.* Whatever decisions we come to should reflect his preferences, even when he gives no detailed guidance. The longer you spend in someone else's company, the more you get to know what their thoughts, feelings, likes, dislikes and preferences are. In the Bible, God has poured himself out to us; he shares his heart, mind, priorities, plans and moral values. Spend time reading the Bible. The more we do, the more our own thought processes and decision-making will be shaped by the mind of God.
- *Constant exposure to the Bible sharpens our own value system*, through its powerful stories, models, examples and direct teaching. This will influence the moral choices we have to make. Think about it. Most of us have mental pictures of what a "good" driver or teacher or parent should be like. These pictures are built up out of hundreds of stories, examples and personal experiences. We use these to construct our ideal model of such people – even if the real ones we know (including ourselves) fall short of the ideal. Similarly, it is from the many stories in the Bible, positive and negative, inspiring and disturbing, that God shapes our instinctive understanding of what is right and good in different circumstances and relationships.
- *The Bible sharpens our sense of sin*, and its teachings and stories gives clear warnings of what sin ends up doing to us. So we become more sensitive to the possible outcomes of the different courses of action available to us. (In 1 Corinthians 10:1–13 Paul highlights this particular aspect of the Bible's function.)
- *The Bible provides good soil for the work of the Holy Spirit in our minds.* A mind that is already well soaked in the Scriptures will be more in tune with the Spirit's leading.

- Can you give specific examples of how the Bible has functioned effectively in guiding particular decisions or actions in the past?

---

b. Guidance or a blueprint (vv. 101, 104, 128)

The psalmist seems to have been a relatively young person in a position of public leadership. Such responsibility could have brought many temptations and involved many choices. But it is interesting to note that when the psalmist talks about God's guidance, he tends to focus more on the negative (avoiding wrong paths) than on the positive (the *only* possible right way).

Take a look at some examples.

> I have kept my feet from every evil path
>   so that I might obey your word. (v. 101)

> I gain understanding from your precepts;
>   therefore I hate every wrong path. (v. 104)

> because I consider all your precepts right,
>   I hate every wrong path. (v. 128)

It seems that the psalmist is already walking on a good path simply by living as a faithful believer in obedience to God's word. He does not ask God for a detailed blueprint for every choice he has to make. He doesn't say, "God, please show me what to do every day." He is walking in the Lord's way, but he still speaks of "my steps," "my feet" and "my path." He still makes his own choices and decisions and looks for negative guidance. We could say that he is looking for red lights or "No Entry" signs rather than for a specific instruction to "turn left here."

We need to be careful about our theology of guidance. Many ideas that are common in Christian circles are not necessarily founded on a clear teaching of the Bible. We are often told that "God has a wonderful plan for your life." Those of us who know the Bible well might question this statement when we remember the many people in the Bible whose lives were turned upside down or virtually wrecked when God got involved in them. Or we are told, "It's all mapped out to the last detail. All you have to do is find out God's plan for your life." Well, we are allowed to ask God many questions, but we don't always get the sort of direct answers we would like when it comes to details. This teaching also leads to our living in fear that if we take a wrong step we will be out of God's will, or at best, have to live with God's second best, his "Plan B." I'm not at all sure that this type of thinking is what the Bible is speaking of when it talks of God's sovereign purpose or his promise to guide his people.

At the opposite extreme is the view that says, "It's really entirely up to you. God has no more idea about what you will do with your life than you have. But if you make good choices, God will come alongside and help you through."

He is as keen to find out what direction you will take and where you will end up as you are." Again, I'm not at all convinced that this is an adequate way to describe the relationship between our free choices and the will of God.

Both the approaches described above are distortions of the true biblical teaching about the openness of the future and the personal and responsive relationship between God and people. The first view stresses that God is sovereign and has a plan, but leaves us groping around trying (and frequently failing) to find out the details of that plan. The second view may also acknowledge that God is sovereign, but it insists that he has no plan, leaving us lost at sea without a rudder or compass. So what should we do?

The Bible certainly teaches these truths:

- God is sovereign over all that happens in the universe and over all history on earth;
- God has a will and purpose that he is working out and will bring to final completion;
- God promises to lead and guide his people;
- God does lead and guide his people.

But there is little evidence in the Bible for the idea that there is an individualized blueprint, absolutely fixed in advance, for every person's life, especially if this leads to the fatalistic view that our lives run to a predetermined script.

Nor is there biblical evidence for the idea that God has one perfect plan or blueprint for our lives, and that if we make a wrong decision we are deviating from this plan and will end up having to settle for Plan B. I remember George Verwer, founder of Operation Mobilization, saying that, if this idea was true, he was glad there were 26 letters in the English alphabet since he must be up to Plan X or Y by now. But is it true? We know, of course, that David speaks of God's foreknowledge of his words and actions, and says that "all the days ordained for me were written in your book" (Ps 139:3–4, 16), but it seems that what he is speaking of is God's intimate knowledge of him and the length of time he would be alive, rather than God's having a detailed blueprint for him to follow each day. If he thought that he was following a blueprint, David went about the matter in some strange ways.

This blueprint model of guidance causes two main problems:

First, it can be the source of great pastoral damage and distress. Every now and then I meet someone who tells me their sad life story: "At the age of twenty-four I disobeyed God and missed his plan for my life, and I've been condemned to second best ever since." Now undoubtedly people do go astray and make a mess of their lives. But the God of the Bible is forever seeking to bring people back into relationship again, back to commissioning, service and fruitfulness. Think of Elijah. Think of Peter. God restores the years the locusts have eaten. He is the God who weaves even our mistakes and foolishness into his sovereign plan and in all things "works for the good of those who love him, who have been called according to his purpose" (Rom 8:28). The blueprint model of guidance generates a great deal of unnecessary anxiety in people who are desperately afraid they might miss some fine point of the future plan, and in people who are desperately afraid that they have already lost the plot somewhere in the past.

Second, the blueprint model of guidance reduces God to a heavenly puppeteer and reduces humanity to puppets controlled by mechanical means. In other words, it removes the "personhood" of God from his sovereignty, and it removes the "personhood" of humanity in our decision-making. Both are serious misconceptions. God relates to us as our heavenly Father, not as our heavenly day-planner. And it is part of the parenting process to bring your children to the maturity of making their own choices and decisions with wisdom and integrity. God has given us minds so we can think, consciences so that we can morally discriminate, and wills so that we can put our own plans into action. He expects us to use them, in prayerful conversation with him and in "the fear of the Lord," with the determination to do only what is consistent with his known character and general will.

God's word then, to return to Psalm 119, is certainly a light for our path. But it does not pre-decide every step and every choice that we have to make. What we need, therefore, is not just light so that we can see where we are going and avoid wrong or dangerous paths, but also discernment. We need constantly maturing insight and understanding that will enable us to make wise and good decisions that are pleasing to God and the best decisions for ourselves and others. That, too, is what the psalmist prays for. And that is what we shall look at in the next chapter.

- What wrong paths should we hate and "keep our feet from" today? Are there any paths we need to turn from now?

- Think about people you know who are having to make big decisions. It could be a decision involving their family, job or home. Reflect on how they must be feeling and bring any particular prayer requests to your group. Then pray together for some of the people you have mentioned.

Further Study

Read Psalm 32.

What clear promise does God make in 32:8–9? What is the first condition for being guided by God (32:1–7)? What is the second condition in 32:8–9?

If the difference between horses and mules and humans is that horses and mules "have no understanding" (32:8), what does this tell us about how God will guide us? And what does this verse tell us about how we should not expect God to guide us?

Reflection and Response

Review the last year. Can anyone in the group give specific examples of how the Bible has functioned effectively in guiding particular decisions or actions in the past?

Consider how you would preach this psalm in a way that encourages people to seek God's guidance while warning them against expecting it to come in the "mechanical" kind of way we use to get a horse to turn left or right or stop.

4

Learning for the Pupil

> **AIM: To assess our willingness to let God's word shape our thinking**

Focus on the Theme

In the last chapter, the psalmist was thinking of God's word as a lamp that we use as we walk along a path on a dark night. But in this chapter, we will be looking at a different metaphor, in which God is our teacher and the Bible is our textbook.

Read: Psalm 119:26–27, 33–34, 97–104
Key verse: Psalm 119:33
Outline

1. God the teacher (vv. 98–100, 102)
2. "Teach me" (vv. 12, 26, 33, 64, 68, 124, 135, 171)
   a. Teaching and praise (vv. 12, 171)
   b. Teaching and practical life and obedience (vv. 26, 33)
   c. Teaching and God's character and action (vv. 64, 68, 124, 135)
3. "Give me understanding" (vv. 27, 34, 73, 104, 125, 144, 169)
   a. Understanding and God as Creator (vv. 27, 73)
   b. Understanding and moral obedience as Creator (vv. 34, 104)
   c. Understanding and a personal relationship with God (vv. 125, 144, 169)

Some years ago, I saw a television advert that showed the faces of a series of celebrities (sport heroes, entertainers, politicians, etc.). Each one said just the name of some unknown person: "Mrs Jones," "Mr Campbell," "Miss Rutherford" and so on. Then came the punch line: *"Nobody forgets a good teacher!"* And it's true. We all remember the few really excellent teachers we have had. The psalmist also remembers his teacher – God. He often speaks of God as his teacher and describes God's word as teaching or instruction. And he does not hesitate to express his appreciation for his teacher!

Let us join him in sitting with a teacher learning, studying, interacting, absorbing, memorizing, reflecting and applying what the teacher shares with us.

- Who have been the good teachers in your life? Why were they good? What difference did they make to your learning? Reflect on some of the qualities that you think make a good teacher.

1. God the Teacher (vv. 98–100, 102)

When the Bible is our textbook, then God himself is our teacher:

> I have not departed from your laws,
> *for you yourself have taught me.* (v. 102, italics added)

Timothy used similar language when writing to Timothy. Timothy had been well-taught as a child by his mother and grandmother. What a blessing and privilege that was! But Paul emphasizes that it was the Scriptures that led him to salvation and provided him with education in righteousness and justice:

> From infancy you have known the Holy Scriptures, which are able to make you wise for salvation through faith in Christ Jesus. All Scripture is God-breathed and is useful for teaching, rebuking, correcting and training in righteousness. (2 Tim 3:15–16)

Indeed, our psalmist reckons that with God as his teacher and the Scriptures as his textbook, he has greater understanding than even his human teachers and his elders (not to mention his enemies).

> Your commands are always with me
>   and make me wiser than my enemies.
> I have more insight than all my teachers,
>   for I meditate on your statutes.

> I have more understanding than the elders,
>> for I obey your precepts. (vv. 98–100)

Perhaps you've heard of the university professor who told a new lecturer that if there was anything she didn't understand she should ask the first year students as soon as possible while they still knew everything about everything. Now, what the psalmist says may sound similar to the exaggerated confidence of youth, but I would hesitate to accuse him of arrogance when he makes these claims. He is not so much making claims about his own knowledge as expressing confidence in the surpassing value and wisdom of the teaching of God in his word.

Working through the psalm while thinking of God as our teacher and his word as our textbook, I noticed that two phrases kept cropping up: "*Teach me your decrees*" occurs eight times and "Give me *understanding/discernment*" (or a similar expression) is used seven times. So for the rest of the chapter let's look at these phrases in the context of the passages in which they occur.

- If we are Christians, we believe with the psalmist that the Bible gives greater insight and understanding than all other education. How is this different from anti-intellectualism?

---

2. "Teach Me" (vv. 12, 26, 33, 64, 68, 124, 135, 171)

As we look at the psalmist's requests for God to teach him, we find varying emphases, almost as if different threads are being woven into the tapestry. Here we will focus on the links between teaching and praise, teaching and practical life and obedience, and teaching and God's character and action.

a. Teaching and praise (vv. 12, 171)

The first point that needs to be made is that the psalmist's prayer "teach me" is closely linked to praise. Both the first and the last time he says "teach me" in this psalm, it is the context of praising God:

> Praise be to you, LORD;
>> teach me your decrees. (v. 12)

> May my lips overflow with praise,
>> for you teach me your decrees. (v. 171)

The psalmist does not separate his head and heart, his theology and his praise, or the intellectual and the spiritual aspects of his life. He does not draw a neat line between worship of God (praise, thanksgiving, singing) and being taught by God. For him, learning leads to overflowing praise.

The same direct link between teaching and praise is found in Nehemiah 8. There we read that the people stood and listened to the law of God being read and taught to them for a whole week. And they wept. And then they rejoiced. And the main reason for their rejoicing was that, through the teaching of the Levites, they now understood the words that were being read to them (Neh 8:12). Paul makes a similar point when he urges the Corinthian believers not to get so carried away with their worship in the Spirit that they forget the importance of feeding the mind also (1 Cor 14:14–19).

It is tragic when Christians separate devotional life, or so-called "worship time," from learning and understanding God's word, or even treat them as if they are to be set in contrast to one another. Both are crucially important. This psalmist longs to be taught so that he can worship and praise God better.

- What are the more common things that we praise God for? Did anyone in the group mention his teaching? If not, or if it was not high on the list, what does this show about what is important to us and what we are grateful for?

---

b. Teaching and practical life and obedience (vv. 26, 33)

The second point to be made is that the psalmist's prayer for God to teach him is linked to practical life and obedience.

> I gave an account of my ways and you answered me;
>   teach me your decrees. (v. 26)

> Teach me, LORD, the way of your decrees,
>   that I may follow it to the end. (v. 33)

We sometimes talk about being accountable to each other for our words and actions. In verse 26 the psalmist mentions his accountability to God.

- Do we give an account at the end of each day? Discuss the way in which this might affect our motivation in studying Scripture.

c. Teaching and God's character and action (vv. 64, 68, 124, 135)

The third point to be made is that the psalmist's prayer is connected to God's character and action.

> The earth is filled with your love, LORD;
>   teach me your decrees. (v. 64)

> You are good, and what you do is good;
>   teach me your decrees. (v. 68)

> Deal with your servant according to your love
>   and teach me your decrees. (v. 124)

> Make your face shine on your servant
>   and teach me your decrees. (v. 135)

Many consider God's *law* as the opposite of his *love*. In the Old Testament, however, God's law was considered one of the supreme gifts of God's grace to the people he loved and redeemed out of slavery. The idea that studying the law was an exercise in dry legalism would have been utterly shocking to this psalmist. It was nothing of the kind. It was an intimate, personal lesson with his gracious divine teacher. The psalmist is saying to God, "Lord, I want *you*, you personally and you only, to be my teacher, because of your goodness, your love and your gracious personal presence with me."

Earlier I said that "everyone remembers a good teacher." The psalmist wants to learn from this teacher because he is good and loving. More than that, he is present with his pupil, for the "face" of God means the presence of God, who is right there in the classroom.

- What difference should it make to our Bible study if we remember that it is being done in the presence of our good and loving teacher?

- You, or your group, are involved in Bible study right now. God is your teacher, because it is his word you are studying. How can this Bible study result in praise, obedience and celebration of the character of God?

- If you are a preacher, how can you preach in such a way that, even though you are teaching your congregation, they can see that you are not like a headmaster but are simply a pupil in God's school, letting God teach you too from his word?

3. "Give Me Understanding" (vv. 27, 34, 73, 104)

In Hebrew "understanding" means insight and discernment, seeing more deeply than just your eyes do. It is the ability to see beneath the surface of things. It is the practical wisdom that comes with maturity and experience, but it can also be taught and learned to some degree. Above all, it is a gift of God that we should pray for. Indeed, in the New Testament, wisdom is listed among the gifts of the Spirit (1 Cor 12:8).

Like his prayer for teaching, the psalmist's prayer for understanding weaves together threads to form a tapestry.

a. Understanding and God as Creator (vv. 27, 73)

The first thread is that understanding is closely associated with God as Creator.

> Cause me to understand the way of your precepts,
> that I may meditate on your wonderful deeds. (v. 27)

> Your hands made me and formed me;
> give me understanding to learn your commands. (v. 73)

The suggestion here is that understanding God's moral teaching comes *before* we consider his creation.

- Consider what the above sentence implies about the relationship between religion/ethics and science?

b. Understanding and moral obedience (vv. 34, 104)

Understanding is closely linked to moral obedience, and especially to avoiding wrong.

> Give me understanding, so that I may keep your law
> and obey it with all my heart. (v. 34)

> I gain understanding from your precepts;
> therefore I hate every wrong path. (v. 104)

The whole point of *learning* from God is to *live* for God. Compare the verses above with Proverbs 1:1–7.

- How has society undermined this order of priority by substituting intellectual and academic wisdom (or technological wizardry) for moral discernment?
- Can you give examples of times when your growth in Christian understanding helped you to reject and avoid making a wrong turn or decision?

c. Understanding and a personal relationship with God (vv. 125, 144, 169)

The psalmist closely links understanding and a personal relationship with God.

> I am your servant; give me discernment
> that I may understand your statutes. (v. 125)

> Your statutes are always righteous;
> give me understanding that I may live. (v. 144)

> May my cry come before you, LORD;
> give me understanding according to your word. (v. 169)

These verses underline a point I made in the Introduction to this book. This is not a psalm about the law itself. Rather, it is about a personal relationship with God. The psalmist's longing is for growth in understanding, that is, for the intellectual and moral wisdom that flows from a relationship with God. God, in these verses, is a Master, a Life-giver and a Helper. The psalmist is simply God's servant. He needs God to give him life and he is needy enough to cry out for help.

- What part does humility play in gaining biblical understanding?
- What part does humility play in asking God to help you understand a Bible text in order to preach it well? And how do you stay humble when God answers your prayer?

Further Study

Read 1 Corinthians 1:24–30.

How does the psalmist's longing for teaching and understanding relate to Paul's statement that all wisdom is available to us through our relationship with God in Christ?

Reflection and Response

Why is it misleading to follow a sermon with words like "And now the band is going to lead us into a time of worship"? What does this imply? What has this psalm taught you about how we should view worship?

Conclude this study by spending some time in prayer, worshipping God for who he is and what he has done.

Section 3

Personal Sin and the Word of Grace

Psalm 119:9–16

Personal Sin and the Word of Grace

Introduction to Section 3

John Bunyan wrote a book called *Pilgrim's Progress* in which a man called Christian sets out on a journey with a heavy burden of sin strapped to his back. He longs to get rid of this load, but it is immovable. So he struggles on enduring all kinds of hardship, until he eventually comes to the foot of the cross. There, in a dramatic moment, his burden of sin falls off and rolls away down the hill and into a great hole, never to be seen again.

Some of the psalms paint a similar picture of the heavy weight of sin. The writer of Psalm 32, for example, vividly describes how he felt dry, crushed and wasted for as long as he lived with unconfessed sin in his life. When he tried to cover it up, it ate at him from the inside. But when he uncovered it to God, then God could cover it with his forgiving grace.

Psalm 51 is probably the most extended confession of sin in the whole book of Psalms. It contains profound reflections, deep penitence and searching prayers for cleansing and restoration. Such psalms arise from profound conviction, usually in the wake of some specific sin. The writers cry out in repentance and are broken in spirit. Such times are intensely painful, but by God's grace they can also be wonderfully restoring and filled with fresh hope. Godly repentance leads to God's forgiveness, and there is indescribable joy in belonging to the fellowship of the forgiven.

Even though Psalm 119 is not really a confession psalm, it is still concerned about sin. The writer is not desperately sorry because he *has* sinned; he is desperately anxious that he *does not* sin. Perhaps this concern arises out of earlier experiences, similar to those that lie behind Psalms 32 and 51. Knowing what it had been like to have to cry out for mercy and wish more than anything to undo the past, the psalmist is determined not to end up there again. So what we find in this psalm is not so much a *confession* of sin as a *consciousness* of sin and a strong determination to do all he can to avoid it.

In the chapters of this section we shall look at the psalmist's awareness of sin and what it does to one, at his strategy for avoiding sin, and at the remarkable answer to sin that we find from this Old Testament believer who knew nothing about Jesus and the cross.

5

Awareness of Sin

> **AIM: To deepen our awareness of the effects of sin in our lives**

Focus on the Theme

Jesus takes sin very seriously. If you doubt this, read Matthew 18:7–9 where he tell us, with a graphic imaginary comparison, that it would be better to be maimed than to simply keep on sinning. His words challenge us – do we view our own sins seriously enough? Do we try and justify "small" sins? At the start of this chapter, take time to pray and ask God to increase your sensitivity to sin. Then as you read and reflect on the verses below, consider whether God is speaking directly to you about a particular area in your life.

Read: Psalm 119:129–136
Key verse: Psalm 119:133
Outline

1. Sin leads to shame and disgrace (vv. 6, 31, 39)
2. Sin leads you astray (vv. 67, 101, 104, 128)
3. Sin eventually rules and dominates your life (v. 133)

How does the psalmist assess the seriousness of sin? What does sin do to people? In this chapter we are going to look at the awareness of sin under the following three headings: sin leads to shame and disgrace, sin leads you astray, and sin eventually rules and dominates lives.

1. Sin Leads to Shame and Disgrace (vv. 6, 31, 39)

> Then I would not be put to shame
> when I consider all your commands. (v. 6)
>
> I hold fast to your statutes, LORD;
> do not let me be put to shame. (v. 31)
>
> Take away the disgrace I dread,
> for your laws are good. (v. 39)

We tend to associate shame with reports in the newspapers of teachers who have been disgraced, of politicians who have been leading a double life, or of children who have brought shame on the family name.

Shame was the first response to sin. In the garden of Eden, Adam and Eve tried to cover themselves and to hide from God. Shame is the urgent desire to be covered, to hide away from the gaze of others. It happens when you are found out and fear being put to shame – especially in cultures where loss of face is something to be avoided at all costs. Other psalms also express this fear of being put to shame. Read, for example, Psalm 25:1–2, 20. The psalmist wants God to protect him from the public shaming that would come about if he were falsely accused and people believed the accusations.

But real sin (not just false accusation) should produce shame. There is a proper inward shame that we ought to feel when we stand uncovered before God and know our own hearts. It is when people can sin without shame that they are in a serious spiritual state of hardness.

Part of the suffering of crucifixion was the public shame it inflicted on the victim. Normally, the victim was crucified naked, making the public exposure even worse. So for Jesus the cross involved not only bearing our sin but also bearing our shame. That is to say, he took upon himself the heaped-up scorn, shame and abuse that should have been ours. One of the two thieves recognized this, while the other simply joined in the abuse.

This dimension of the cross only impacted me when, on one occasion, I came to profound repentance for behaviour that had been well hidden. If it had come into the open, I would have been disgraced. As I brought my sin to the cross for forgiveness, I suddenly realized that the shame I should and would have known was indeed taken by Jesus. Not only did I find forgiveness and cleansing in the blood of Christ, but also protection from shame – just as the psalmists prayed. It was deeply humbling and deeply reassuring.

> Bearing shame and scoffing rude,
> *in my place* condemned He stood;
> Sealed my pardon with His blood;
> Hallelujah! what a Saviour![1] (italics added)

Today the whole idea of sin has become fairly meaningless to many people. The loss of any awareness of a transcendent personal God to whom we are morally accountable has led to a loss of any sense of guilt in having offended him or having done wrong in some objective sense. In its place there is a sense of shame. But even that is not the same as the biblical sense of shame, namely shame in the presence of God. It is more an inner shame about the gap between the "persona" we project (our external image that is supported by the stories we tell about ourselves and our posts on social media) and the person we know ourselves to be on the inside. We are, literally, ashamed of "our-selves."

One of the challenges facing us in communicating the liberating gospel of the Bible is how to respond to this cultural phenomenon. The familiar terms we use as Christians may not make any sense in the world outside. How are we going to find ways of communicating the truth of what the Bible says in language and concepts that do make sense?

- What kind of disgrace do you think the psalmist was afraid of and how is that relevant to us today?

- How do you think we should address the problem of a lack of a sense of sin and the presence of a twisted sense of shame in our society?

---

2. Sin Leads You Astray (vv. 67, 101, 104, 128)

We have already seen that one of the favourite pictures for the life of a believer in this psalm is that of a path, or a way. The psalmist wants God to guide him in good and right ways. Equally, the psalmist wants to avoid taking the wrong

---

1. From the hymn "Man of Sorrows, what a name" by Philip Bliss.

path. And sin always puts us on the wrong path. When we deliberately do what we know is displeasing to God, it puts us on a wrong track, and that tends to lead to another wrong track (as we try to cover up the first sin), and then to another, until we end up far away from where God wants us to be. Look at some of the verses where the psalmist wants to avoid that fate.

> Before I was afflicted I went astray,
> but now I obey your word. (v. 67)

> I have kept my feet from every evil path
> so that I might obey your word. (v. 101)

In verse 67 the psalmist suggests that his afflictions (his sufferings) have stopped him going astray; now he is determined to be obedient:

> I gain understanding from your precepts;
> therefore I hate every wrong path. (v. 104)

> and because I consider all your precepts right,
> I hate every wrong path. (v. 128)

Wrong paths, of course, can also be dangerous paths. Once we know we are on a wrong path, the best thing to do is to turn back and retrace our steps. Sin always starts with one step; it then becomes a series of steps that lead us further down the wrong path. The further we go, the harder it becomes to turn back at all. So this psalmist's wise advice is to do our best to avoid that first step.

- Can you think of any times in your own life when afflictions or sufferings have brought you back in line with God's word? Discuss these with the group.
- "I hate every wrong path." How can we cultivate this sort of attitude without becoming self-righteous as we do so?

---

3. Sin Eventually Rules and Dominates Your Life (v. 133)

Sin becomes a hard master and we end up enslaved to it. This is exactly what God told Cain that sin would do (Gen 4:7). Here our theology matches our personal experience. As a friend of mine who worked with drug abusers says, "When it comes to sin, we are all recovering addicts." Sin has an addictive ability to overpower us and take us captive. The Bible warns us about this. Only the power of God can deliver us, and then protect us.

So one reason why our psalmist prays for God to keep him on the right path is so that he will avoid being ruled and dominated by sin.

> Direct my footsteps according to your word;
> let no sin rule over me. (v. 133)

- What additional insights on this verse can you find in Romans 6:11–14?

- In what ways does the "rule of sin" reveal itself in our lives?

- If you are a preacher, are you careful when preaching about sin to your congregation to be fully aware of the presence of sin in your own life, and are you as aware of its dangers as this psalmist was? Only as repentant and forgiven sinners can we preach to others.

Realistic and Radical

The Bible has a great deal more to say on the subject of sin in many other places, including other psalms. And thinking about our own experience as sinners should easily and quickly indicate many other ways in which we fall.

We should not take our failure lightly. The Bible expects us to be realistic and radical in our attitude to sin. We need to constantly remind ourselves that sin makes great promises, but fails to deliver on all of them.

- Sin promises fun and excitement, but it delivers pain and tragedy.
- Sin promises freedom, but it delivers slavery and addiction.
- Sin promises life and fulfilment, but it delivers emptiness, frustration and death.
- Sin promises gain, but it delivers loss.
- Sin promises that we can get away with it, but the fact is we don't.

Psalm 119 comes with a sober warning. Be aware of the reality of sin and what it does in human life. Acknowledge and face up to these things. Be real about yourself.

Further Study

Read Psalm 51.

Read Psalm 51 prayerfully, joining David in this prayer for God to renew and refresh us. Are there particular areas in your life that you need to bring before God?

Reflection and Response

Finish this chapter with confession of sin and a prayer of thankfulness to God for the reality of his forgiveness in Christ. Sin is serious, but as Christians we know that ultimately our sin can be fully dealt with at the cross of Christ. Let this concluding thought shape your prayers and response to God now.

6

Avoiding Sin: Strengthening Our Minds and Wills

> **AIM: To strengthen our resistance to sin and our faith in God's mercy**

Focus on the Theme

Ephesians 6:10–18 uses battle imagery and exhorts us to put on the "full armour of God." Read those verses and keep those images in mind as you read this chapter. Avoiding sin is not something we can do passively; it requires action on our part.

Read: Psalm 119:9–16

Key verse: Psalm 119:11

Outline

1. Exercising our minds (vv. 9, 11, 13 and 15)
2. Exercising our wills (vv. 30, 101, 106, 112)

How can we resist sin? The Bible tells us that sin deeply affects the whole human person.

> The LORD saw how great the wickedness of the human race had become on the earth, and that every inclination of the thoughts of the human heart was only evil all the time. (Gen 6:5)

There is no part of the human personality that is unspoilt by sin. The physical, spiritual, intellectual, emotional, intentional and relational dimensions of human life are all twisted and distorted by its infection. Chapters 3 to 11 of Genesis vividly show what this means (see also Rom 1:18–32; 2:9).

So if every part of us is affected by sin, we have to involve every part of ourselves in resisting it. And that is exactly what we find the psalmist doing. As we read his words, we can see different tactics he uses in his struggle to avoid temptation and sin. Let's analyse the psalmist's strategy and see what it has to teach us in our own battles. In this chapter we shall think about exercising our minds and wills. And in the following chapter, we shall think about strengthening our emotions and our faith – all with the aim of avoiding sin.

1. Exercising Our Minds (vv. 9, 11, 13, 15)

The psalm is filled, as we have seen again and again, with references to the word of God. And the writer tells us that he spends a lot of time and energy *thinking* about God's word. He does not see this just as an academic exercise; he has the specific goal of avoiding sin and keeping his feet on the right path. In fact the whole of the second stanza of the poem (vv. 9–16) deals with this, beginning with the question we are considering.

> How can a young person stay on the path of purity?
>   By living according to your word. (v. 9)

The second line of this verse, the answer to the psalmist's question, could be translated more literally as "*By watching it* according to your word." It means bringing every step we make in life, every choice and decision, every opportunity or temptation under the judgement of God's word and asking "What does the Bible say?"

> I have hidden your word in my heart
>   that I might not sin against you. (v. 11)
>
> With my lips I recount
>   all the laws that come from your mouth. (v. 13)
>
> I meditate on your precepts
>   and consider your ways. (v. 15)

The psalmist does not just list or talk about God's laws; he also meditates on them and hides them in his heart. If you skim through the psalm you will find many more indications that he is determined to give to the Scripture the serious mental attention it deserves. The psalmist is clearly *thinking* about God's word. And he isn't just thinking about it so that he can come up with a few pious songs to soothe his heart. No, he is studying the Bible regularly and carefully and is finding great joy and delight in his study, which is as it should be.

Why does he give such priority to studying God's law? He believes that by continually deepening his knowledge of the Scripture he will strengthen his ability to avoid sinning. If we were to use a modern metaphor, we could even say that he regards God's word as a kind of disinfectant to get rid of the germs of sin. Below are some of the ways in which it does this.

- The Bible keeps us more in touch with the mind of God. This means that the more we know it, the more sensitive we are to sin. We become more alert to God's priorities, and do not just accept the prejudices or legalism of the tradition we belong to.
- The Bible includes many examples of the types of temptations we are exposed to. These examples are there for our benefit. So as we read the Bible, we should be asking "Is there an example to follow or an error to avoid?" The stories in the Bible have great teaching power as they develop our awareness of sin, or what we could call our "sin-sensors."
- The Bible gives us a strong weapon against temptation. Paul described the word of God as "the sword of the Spirit" (Eph 6:17). The more we fill our hearts and minds with Spirit-inspired Scriptures, the more we will be ready to fight the battles ahead.
- The Bible ruthlessly unmasks our pretences. It is "sharper than any double-edged sword" (Heb 4:12). One effect of that, in my experience at least, is that the Bible quickly deals with our tendency to explain away and excuse our own sin. As we come up with all kinds of reasons why we couldn't really help it, or why it was really somebody else's fault, the Bible sits there, convicting us: "Who do you think you're kidding? Get real, my friend."
- The Bible warns us. We think, "I can get away with it; nobody knows." And the Bible murmurs, "Be sure . . . your sin will find you out" (Num 32:23).
- The Bible challenges wishful thinking. We think, "God doesn't really mind; he's too nice to make a fuss about what I'm doing." And the Bible responds with a thunderous health warning, "Do not be deceived: God cannot be mocked. A man reaps what he sows" (Gal 6:7).

The more we absorb the Bible into our heart, mind, soul and bloodstream, the harder we will find it to sin comfortably. The Bible awakens our conscience and drives us back to God in repentance and with a longing to live in a way that pleases him. Fill your mind with it as much as you can.

- Discuss how we can meditate on God's word in our personal Bible study and in group study. What does "meditation" involve?
- Can you give examples of how God's word has functioned as a kind of disinfectant in your own life?

2. Exercising Our Wills (vv. 30, 101, 106, 112)

Psalm 119 is full of determination. The psalmist leaves us in no doubt as to what he *wills* to do and not do. He is going to *choose* to do what is good and *choose* not to do what is evil. We have no way of knowing how successful he may or may not have been in keeping his resolutions. The psalmist was human like the rest of us, so no doubt he failed pretty often. But the point is that he was determined to avoid sin, and he knew that he needed to strengthen his will in that direction, as well as exercising his mind by studying the word of God. Read the verses below:

> I have chosen the way of faithfulness;
>   I have set my heart on your laws. (v. 30)

> I have kept my feet from every evil path
>   so that I might obey your word. (v. 101)

Verse 30 displays a positive exercise of the will (what he will do) while verse 101 refers to the negative (what he won't do). He is very clear about what he has chosen to do and is deeply committed to his choice:

> I have taken an oath and confirmed it,
>   that I will follow your righteous laws. (v. 106)

> My heart is set on keeping your decrees
>   to the very end. (v. 112)

If we do not have long-term goals in view, we will end up following our impulses – the first ideas that come to our mind when we wake up and think,

"Well, what am I going to do today?" That is the way many prefer to live. We are afraid of long-term commitments and prefer to take a short-term approach to everything. This makes for some very easy-going forms of Christian living. To set our hearts, that is, our wills, on doing something "to the very end" will mark us as very different from those around us.

It is important to recognize that sin *is* a matter of choice and will. Yes, of course, it is also a matter of temptation, seduction, enticement and sometimes just stumbling over and falling down before we even see the trip wire. But we do not have to fall when temptation comes.

The very first sin recorded in the Bible was an act of choice. After the conversation between the serpent and Eve, in which Eve had been led to question God's motives and doubt his goodness, the serpent plays no further part in the story until summoned by God for judgment. The serpent did not offer Eve a glass of freshly squeezed fruit juice and pour it down her throat. She saw, she thought, she took, she ate, she gave and he ate also. Eve and Adam *chose* to disobey. They were not compelled to do so.

It may sound strange to say so, but you don't have to sin. Let me explain. In saying "you don't have to sin," I do not mean that it is possible for us to be sinless or morally perfect. We *do* sin. We are born into a legacy of sin. We are fallen in Adam and sin is part of our fallen human nature. In fact, as John puts it, if we say we do not sin, we are deceiving ourselves and calling God a liar as well (1 John 1:8–10). But this inborn tendency towards sin does not remove the fact that we are morally responsible for our choices and our actions. The essence of sin is that we deliberately choose to do what we *know* we ought not to do, and not to do what we *know* we ought to do. This is a fact of experience that Paul wrestles with in Romans 7. It is a choice we make; we are not forced to sin. We are not robots or puppets on a string, or even animals acting on instinct. We are morally conscious human persons to whom God has given the gift of choosing, of exercising our own wills.

So for all these reasons, it is vital to strengthen our *wills* in the direction of God's will. Like this psalmist we need to think, to decide, to take steps and to determine what we will and will not do.

Of course we all fail. But that does not mean there is no point in making the effort and praying for God to work within us to mould our will to his. The Holy Spirit is a gentle persuader, working within us so that we will what he wills and choose what he would choose.

A biblical example may help here. What did Joseph do when faced with sexual temptation? He resisted it, explaining his refusal to sin by explaining his priorities and his commitment to Potiphar, his benefactor and master, and to God. Joseph's determination stood firm, despite being tempted "day after day." So when the temptation was repeated with urgent physical appeal, he made an urgent physical exit (Gen 39:7–12).

The earlier you take a stand, the stronger you become to face harder tests later. A young friend of mine is an accountant in training. A senior partner in the firm asked him to sign off on some accounts that contained irregularities. His conscience was stirred: he knew he couldn't agree to such work ethics. But if he refused, it might endanger his chances of success and a good reference for future employment. He and I talked about his dilemma and looked at the numerous Bible texts that speak of the supreme value that God puts on integrity and honesty, and the cost involved in living by that standard.

Of course, we sometimes fail to stick to our resolutions, and the Bible is honest in recording failures as well as successes. Peter, like all the disciples, said he would never deny Jesus but would die with him if necessary. Yet all the disciples except Peter and John abandoned Jesus and fled, and then Peter denied that he even knew Jesus. His good resolutions had lasted about three hours. What a failure! But the answer to Peter's failure of will and nerve at that point lay in Jesus's restoring love and recommissioning after the resurrection. Peter the failure became Peter the forgiven, and the same Peter, out of that experience, writes to the rest of us in his two epistles.

- Discuss what "choosing the way of faithfulness" means. How does this relate to your own personal experience and circumstances?

- Which do you think is more difficult: positive obedience or negative avoidance? Why?

- In verse 106 the psalmist talks about having taken an "oath." Can you think of an appropriate cultural equivalent for us?

- Read Daniel 1. How did Daniel and his friends resolve to honour God and at what cost?

Further Study

Read 1 Peter 5:8–10.

What does Peter say we have to do and what does he promise that God will do? A parallel passage to consider is James 4:7–10. Note that both passages involve our wills. We exercise them, and God strengthens them.

Reflection and Response

Have there been times for you when resisting temptation came down to sheer willpower and choosing against the odds to do the right thing? What was the cost? What was the result?

7

Avoiding Sin: Strengthening Our Emotions and Faith

AIM: To encourage our faith in God's compassion and mercy

Focus on the Theme

In chapter 6 we looked at how the challenge of avoiding sin includes exercising our *minds* on the word of God and exercising our *wills* to bring our choices and actions into line with the will of God. But the writer of Psalm 119 is not just a cold intellectual, with a head stuffed full of the Bible and sound doctrine. Nor is the psalmist just a cold disciplinarian, with great self-control of an iron will. On the contrary, the psalmist *feels* very deeply and does not hesitate to express some very strong emotions. In this chapter we will look at our response to sin through our emotions and our faith.

Read: Psalm 119:73–80, 153–160

Key verse: Psalm 119:132

Outline

1. Exercising our emotions (vv. 53, 104, 128, 136, 158, 163)
2. Exercising our faith (vv. 11, 29, 41, 76, 77, 132)

The book of Revelation contains a strong warning about the dangers of being emotionally lukewarm Christians (Rev 3:15–17). But how can we avoid this danger? One way is to learn from the psalmist and exercise our emotions so that we still feel strongly about our sins, and the other is to exercise faith in what God does about sin.

1. Exercising Our Emotions (vv. 53, 104, 128, 136, 158, 163)

Among the psalmist's strongest, deepest and most frequently expressed emotions is his reaction to sin and evil. As you read the verses below, use your own words to describe how he feels.

> Indignation grips me because of the wicked,
>   who have forsaken your law. (v. 53)

> I gain understanding from your precepts;
>   therefore I hate every wrong path. (v. 104, see also v. 128)

> Streams of tears flow from my eyes,
>   for your law is not obeyed. (v. 136)

> I look on the faithless with loathing,
>   for they do not obey your word. (v. 158)

> I hate and detest falsehood
>   but I love your law. (v. 163)

Here are some strong emotions! Part of the reason for such strong feelings could be that the psalmist's mind is so filled with the Scriptures that it echoes or mirrors some of God's own feelings and attitudes towards sin. The prophets do the same thing. All the feelings of God come out in their words: his anger, grief, disbelief, disgust, sense of betrayal, frustration, even his longing for better times and better things.

We may be inclined to disapprove when we hear the psalmist expressing such sentiments. But isn't it right to feel that way about sin and evil, if that is how God feels about them? We are called to share God's hatred of wickedness without falling into hatred and abuse of the people involved. That is the difficulty. Ought we not to pray more that God would increase our sensitivity to our own sin?

If we can sin without being bothered by it, we have seriously lost touch with the heart of God. But if the word of God fills our hearts and minds, then our emotions will also be affected by the feelings of God's heart. That will result in some kind of emotional reaction to sin, both in ourselves and in the world.

But does all this suggest that Psalm 119 is simply just another form of a do-it-yourself course on Christian spirituality? Could we publish it under the title *Sin and How to Avoid It in Three Simple Steps*? So far, it sounds as if all you have to do is read the Bible every day, think positively and keep in touch with your feelings.

But to even suggest that is to totally misunderstand what is going on. The idea that rules alone can solve the problem of sin is legalism, and the psalmist is certainly no legalist. Also, the idea that we can solve the problem of sin by our own efforts is the opposite of what the Bible teaches. It is certainly true that the psalmist wants to do all that he can to *avoid* sinning against God. He is straining every fibre of his mind, his will and his emotions to resist sin. And so should we. But the psalmist also knows that the final answer to sin lies outside himself. And that is why he has to exercise his faith as well as his emotions.

- Read the warning to the church in Laodicea in Revelation 3:15–17. What lessons can we learn from this passage in relation to the way we view our sins? What are the dangers of being an emotionally lukewarm Christian?

---

2. Exercising Our Faith (vv. 11, 29, 41, 76, 77, 132)

In the Introduction I said that Psalm 119 is not primarily about the law but about God, and in particular about the psalmist's own relationship with God. He is not someone who wants to keep the rules because "rules are rules." He tells us why he wants to keep them in verse 11:

> I have hidden your word in my heart
>> that I might not sin against you.

It is his relationship with God that he does not want to be damaged by sin and folly. He knows that when he does sin, the answer must come from God's side of the relationship.

But can there be any hope at all for this psalmist then? Surely this poor Old Testament believer with an Old Testament God will have to wait until the New Testament gets going before he can expect any grace and forgiveness for his sin?

This suggestion reveals a very wrong idea about the Old Testament and the God of the whole Bible! Sadly this common view is sometimes based on a misunderstanding of John 1:17 where John says that "The law was given through Moses; grace and truth came through Jesus Christ." People sometimes place a "but" between the two ideas in that quotation, as if they were in contrast. But they aren't; the second idea adds depth to the first. If we want to add anything between them, it should be "Yes, and . . ." In fact, the translation "grace and truth *came*" is not a good one. John actually says "grace and truth *became*." That is, grace and truth became visible, real and recognizable in the person of Jesus. John is not implying that there was no grace or truth in the Old Testament! Quite the opposite. The gift of the law through Moses was itself an act of God's grace. That's why John says that "we have all received grace in place of grace already given" (John 1:16).

But let's hear the psalmist speaking for himself. Read the following verses, preferably slowly and aloud, and let them sink in. Reflect on how the psalmist describes God's character and attitude.

> Keep me from deceitful ways;
>   be *gracious* to me and teach me your law. (v. 29)

> May your *unfailing love* come to me, LORD,
>   your salvation, according to your promise. (v. 41)

> May your *unfailing love* be my comfort,
>   according to your promise to your servant. (v. 76)

> Let your *compassion* come to me that I may live,
>   for your law is my delight. (v. 77)

> Turn to me and have *mercy* on me,
>   as you always do to those who love your name. (v. 132)

Think about these words. Did you really hear them? He asks God to be "gracious" and speaks of God's "unfailing love," "compassion" and "mercy." Is there anything there that you, as a Christian, do not pray for and rely on when you confess your sins before God? We may do our best to avoid sin, but the only answer to our sin lies in God, and specifically in God's grace, love, salvation, comfort, compassion, mercy and salvation. And these characteristics were exactly what the psalmist and other Old Testament believers knew and loved about the character of God.

How did the psalmist know these things about the Lord, the God of Israel? The answer can be found in verse 29 above where grace and law are talked about in the same breath: "Be gracious to me and teach me your law." But, you ask, how does the law, of all things, reveal the grace and love of God?

To answer this question we need to remember that for the Israelites "the Law" was the Torah: the five books of the Pentateuch, from Genesis to Deuteronomy. In these books, the story that would have told the Israelites the most about God's character was his forgiveness of Israel's rebellion at Sinai when they worshipped the golden calf (Exod 32–34). That story explains the psalmist's understanding of God. It is why he can appeal to God as a God of grace while also speaking of God's law. For it was at Sinai that God first revealed his law to the Israelites, and it was also there that God first revealed his name and his character to Moses in a magnificent declaration that is echoed repeatedly throughout the Bible:

> And he passed in front of Moses, proclaiming, "The LORD, the LORD, the compassionate and gracious God, slow to anger, abounding in love and faithfulness, maintaining love to thousands, and forgiving wickedness, rebellion and sin. Yet he does not leave the guilty unpunished." (Exod 34:6–7)

That is how the "God of the Old Testament" introduces and defines himself.

Now of course we know that ultimately we can only speak of God's righteousness and mercy in the light of the cross. That was where God's character was fully and finally displayed – his wrath and his mercy; his judgment and his grace; his condemnation of sin and his love for sinners.

But Hebrews 11 tells us that the people of faith in the Old Testament are included with us in the great community of those whom God has redeemed through the cross of Christ. And in my imagination, I can see them too looking at that great outpouring of God's self-giving love and saying, "Yes, that is our God. That is what we know that he, and only he, could do. He is the God of love, patience, grace, mercy and forgiveness. We knew that too. And we even gave you the vocabulary to express it. Those were *our* words for God before they became yours. We told you that the answer to the problem of human sin could only lie in the mercy of God himself, and now he has proved his love."

We who are blessed to live after Calvary know the full extent of God's love in history. But I think that nothing can match the language of the Old Testament when it comes to expressing our wonder at the forgiving grace of God. I find myself turning to these great Old Testament texts (such as the ones in the Reflection and Response section below) when I need to come back to God in humble repentance, to hear again the words of inexhaustible grace. Perhaps you would like to do the same.

- Can you think of any other stories in the books from Genesis to Deuteronomy that reveal God's grace and mercy?
- Spend time pondering the majesty and comfort of the psalmist's wonderful statements of faith and then join with him in thanking God for his grace.

Further Study

Reread the crucifixion narrative found in Matthew 27:27–56.

Spend time meditating on what it meant for Jesus to die for us. Come before God, expressing your thanks and gratitude for what he has done for us.

Reflection and Response

Select a few of the Bible references listed below, and spend time by yourself or in a group meditating on what it means to be forgiven by God and how this should affect our lives: Psalm 25:6–11; 32:1–5; 103:8–14; 130:3–4; Isaiah 43:25; 55:6–7; 57:15–18; Ezekiel 18:21–22; 36:25–26; Micah 7:18–19.

As a preacher, after working through these two chapters, how will you preach Bible texts that will help people to be aware of sin and to avoid sin without becoming harshly judgmental or sounding arrogant and perfect yourself? How will you balance the necessity of exposing sin and the necessity of preaching grace?

Section 4

Personal Struggle and the Word of Lament

Psalm 119:81–88

Personal Struggle and the Word of Lament

Introduction to Section 4

In Hebrew the name of the book we call "Psalms" is actually "Praises." So it is somewhat strange that the largest single category of psalms in the book are *laments*! This may be more surprising to us than it was to the Israelites, since we have reduced the word "praise" to meaning bubbly expressions of cheerful thanksgiving and joy. But praise for the Israelites meant more than that. To them, praising God meant acknowledging God's reality and involvement in the whole of life, whatever the circumstances. So, even when life was tough, they would turn to God and lay everything before him, sometimes in protest or lament. This was a form of praise for it was an appeal to the God they knew, loved and trusted, in spite of all the temptations to abandon him and stop worshipping him.

The psalms of lament all tend to go something like this:

- God, I'm hurting
- God, everybody else is attacking and laughing at me
- God, you're not doing much to help right now
- God, I still trust you, but how long will this go on, please?

I suggest you take a quick look at Psalms 35, 43 and 70, which are good examples of this pattern.

Psalm 119 is not strictly a psalm of lament, since it has many other elements woven into it, as we are seeing. But there is a lot of lament in it. Clearly whoever wrote this poem was having a tough time and was struggling with pain, anxiety, fear and confusion. Early in the psalm he says that he feels like a "stranger" on the earth (v. 19), and in the very last verse he still feels like a "lost sheep" (v. 176). So this person is not in a happy and secure state of mind. In the next three chapters, we will be looking at three aspects of his life:

- *His difficulties*. The psalmist had endured contempt, slander and even conspiracies against him.

- *His reactions.* The psalmist was deeply affected by the wickedness he saw in society and paid a steep emotional price.
- *His dual response.* The psalmist saw no contradiction between crying out to God for help and gritting his teeth in determination to carry on.

8

When Life Gets Tough

AIM: To face up to some of the struggles and pressures that believers face

Focus on the Theme

How do you react when the going gets tough? Do you complain, pull a sheet over your head, phone a friend, pray? Changing how we respond and putting our trust in God is sometimes not easy when faced with opposition and abuse, as the psalmist found out.

Read: Psalm 119:19–25, 81–88, 141–147

Key verse: Psalm 119:141

Outline

1. The pain of scorn and contempt (vv. 22, 42, 141)
2. The pain of slander and conspiracy (vv. 23, 69, 78, 84–86, 95, 110, 121, 134, 157, 161)
3. Living with pain

The first clue we get that all is not sunny in this psalmist's life is his statement that he feels like "a stranger on earth" (v. 19). For some reason, he is feeling out of place, as if he does not fit in. As we shall see, that is an understatement. But it is where he starts.

The psalmist seems to have been a young man who was very aware of his inexperience and vulnerability. When he asked, "How can a young person keep his way pure?" (v. 9), he may have been asking a question that concerned him personally. He was aware that others were his teachers and elders (vv. 99, 100). At the same time, he seems to have been involved in some kind of public or political leadership, for he was known by rulers and kings (vv. 23, 46). So perhaps he was a relatively young man who found himself thrust into the public arena, called on to act in a cynical world in which he felt somewhat out of his depth. He was anxious, struggling to maintain his own integrity in the face of much opposition, unsure of his own ability, but eager to maintain his confidence in God and in God's word as the foundation of his life and work.

Does that description sound familiar? It may be how you are feeling, and it may be how other Christians are feeling as they start their careers or enter the rough-and-tumble world of politics. If you are a preacher, you may well have some younger members in your congregation in such a position.

Two things in particular caused the psalmist great pain. These were the contempt with which others treated him and the slanders spread about him.

1. The Pain of Scorn and Contempt (vv. 22, 42, 141)

> Remove from me their scorn and contempt,
>   for I keep your statutes. (v. 22)
>
> Then I can answer anyone who taunts me,
>   for I trust in your word. (v. 42)
>
> Though I am lowly and despised,
>   I do not forget your precepts. (v. 141)

To be laughed at or held in contempt is deeply painful and destructive. And yet it is tragically common. And it starts so young. We wince at the suffering of children who are subjected to physical, verbal or social bullying at school. Some adults have never recovered from the belittling comments they received from their parents, often unfairly comparing them to their brothers or sisters. Others endure mockery at work, or vicious racist or sexist humour and worse.

- Despite being scorned, taunted and despised, the psalmist insists on obeying God's commands and trusting his word. What does this tell us about his character?

---

2. The Pain of Slander and Conspiracy (vv. 23, 69, 78, 84–86, 95, 110, 121, 134, 157, 161)

It gets worse. This person is not just being laughed at; he is apparently also in serious danger, at least some of the time. We become even more aware of this when we read some of the verses on either side of the sad verses quoted below:

> Though rulers sit together and slander me,
> > your servant will meditate on your decrees. (v. 23)

> Though the arrogant have smeared me with lies,
> > I keep your precepts with all my heart. (v. 69)

> May the arrogant be put to shame for wronging me without cause;
> > but I will meditate on your precepts. (v. 78)

> How long must your servant wait?
> > When will you punish my persecutors?
> The arrogant dig pits to trap me,
> > contrary to your law.
> All your commands are trustworthy;
> > help me, for I am being persecuted without cause. (vv. 84–86)

> The wicked are waiting to destroy me,
> > but I will ponder your statutes. (v. 95)

> The wicked have set a snare for me,
> > but I have not strayed from your precepts. (v. 110)

> I have done what is righteous and just;
> > do not leave me to my oppressors. (v. 121)

> Redeem me from human oppression,
> > that I may obey your precepts. (v. 134)

> Many are the foes who persecute me,
> > but I have not turned from your statutes. (v. 157)

> Rulers persecute me without cause,
> > but my heart trembles at your word. (v. 161)

I suppose it is possible that the psalmist is merely paranoid and imagining all this persecution. But more likely, he is telling us the truth about what he is going through. He is having a really tough time. Even today, this type of behaviour is all too familiar to those who are in positions of public and political leadership where back-stabbing, conspiracies, entrapment, unjust accusations and character assassination are occupational hazards.

Daniel knew such a world. He was a civil servant in high government office. There were those who trusted him, and there were those who hated him. And the hatred from his peers and juniors was a mixture of racist and religious prejudice and professional jealousy. When his enemies could find no way to accuse him of corruption or negligence in his work, they engineered his downfall, not through his weakness but through his strongest distinguishing characteristic – his faith.

- Read Daniel 6, noting especially verses 3–5. In what ways is his experience similar to that of the author of Psalm 119? In what ways do both texts speak to your own experience?

3. Living with Pain

We have been thinking about public or political leadership, but any leadership role exposes you to other people's jealousy, misinterpretation and attacks. Christian leadership is no exception. In fact it can sometimes be even worse:

- Pastors and ministers can feel like Moses facing opposition and criticism as they try to lead those who refuse to be led or try to share a vision with those who are determined to be blind.
- Cross-cultural missionaries can endure physical hardship. Many of them live in places where there is religious oppression, and they may experience actual danger or suffer as a result of misinterpretation of their motives.

And it is not just leaders who endure this type of hostility. The words of the psalmist ring true in many other situations, some of which are listed below.

- Christians in a non-Christian family may have to endure much misunderstanding and abuse.
- Christians in hostile workplaces may face discrimination. A stand for honesty or truth-telling can be very unpopular. In countries where another religion dominates society, being a Christian may

rule out any chances of promotion and guarantee a life in which one is constantly harassed and persecuted.
- Christian young people who choose to live their lives in accordance with biblical standards of behaviour, especially in sexual ethics, face a lack of understanding and mocking contempt. There may even be a continued attempt to shame them.

Finally, there are many of us who, while we may not suffer abuse like that which the psalmist describes, can easily understand these words of mockery, taunting, oppression, smearing and lies as they are part of the satanic assault we experience. We know only too well the inner voices that attack us:

- *Fear.* Fear can be exhausting and weakening: "You'll never succeed" or "You'll never get better."
- *Self-accusation.* When we refuse to believe the truth that God says of us, and instead believe all kinds of negative things about ourselves, we cover ourselves with lies.
- *Guilt.* Satan takes advantage of our genuine guilt for real sins and our guilty feelings. So even after we have taken them to the cross, confessed them and been forgiven, the old accuser persecutes us with guilt we no longer need to carry.
- *Self-pity and bitterness.* It is a short step from real and actual suffering of wrong to a constant *feeling* of being wronged and victimized. It becomes a kind of upside-down pride, and since it is very difficult to recognize and repent of, Satan loves it. Satan stirs it up or sets it blazing within us.

You may recognize some of these "enemies." And you may be able to name a few more. But whatever your experience in these things, the psalmist is someone who has walked where you walk, sat where you sit, struggled and wept and protested as you may have done.

- The psalmist was not the only person in the Bible to suffer like this. Jeremiah and Job both suffered so much that they wished they had never been born. Reflect on their examples, and discuss any other examples in the Bible that you can think of.
- How should we pray for Christians in leadership or those with high responsibility? How can we encourage them?

Further Study

Read Jeremiah 15:10, 15–18; 20:7–18 and Job 3.

In what ways does the fact that God allows laments and protests like these to be part of the Bible bring us encouragement in tough times? How can we make more use of such texts as individuals and as a church? In what contexts can we use them?

How can our preaching really enter into the painful experiences of our church members – at home or at work – and address them pastorally from God's word, possibly using some of the sections of this psalm?

Reflection and Response

We should not end this chapter without reference to Jesus. Read 1 Peter 2:20–23 and reflect on how Jesus's example relates to what has been discussed in this chapter and on how this relates to the way the psalmist prays about his problems.

9

How Does It Feel?

AIM: To be honest about our emotional responses to evil

Focus on the Theme

How are you feeling? You could be tired, sad, happy, angry, worried or anxious about a number of things. Why are you feeling like this? Grab a copy of this week's newspaper. How do you react to what you read? Do you have the same intensity of feeling about national and international issues as you do about more personal matters?

Read: Psalm 119:25–28, 81–83, 113–120

Key verse: Psalm 119:136

Outline

1. The evil outside (vv. 21, 53, 113, 115, 118–119, 126, 136, 139, 158)
2. The pain inside (vv. 25, 28, 50, 81–83, 92, 107, 139)

One thing about this psalmist is that we always know exactly how he feels. He doesn't hesitate to express his thoughts and emotions. So we can look at what all the opposition and suffering he is enduring are doing to him emotionally. We will notice two things: his reaction to the evil outside and his response to the pain inside.

The aim of this study is to be as honest with ourselves as this psalmist was with his readers. That in itself is not easy, but it is the first step towards receiving the help we need from God and one another.

1. The Evil Outside (vv. 21, 53, 113, 115, 118–119, 126, 136, 139, 158)

So much of what goes on in the world is nasty, cruel and downright evil. How do we react to all this? What thoughts fill our minds as we read our newspapers or watch the TV news, seeing scene after scene of genocide or brutality, or hearing another sickening account of the sexual abuse of children, or watching in amazement as corrupt politicians who have been caught out in lies and deceit insist that they are innocent victims?

Our psalmist is no passive observer. He is not a cynical reporter gleefully exposing the wickedness of others for his own gain. He is not like those who write lurid headlines about public figures who have been caught in sexual scandals while at the same time publishing articles that encourage lustful fantasies.

On the contrary, the psalmist cares so deeply about God and God's law that he is terribly distressed at the blatant evil and corruption he sees around him. It is almost too painful to bear. You can see this in the verses below. As you read them, reflect on the different emotions he displays and what it is that causes them.

> Indignation grips me because of the wicked,
>   who have forsaken your law. (v. 53)

> I hate double-minded people,
>   but I love your law. (v. 113)

> Away from me, you evildoers,
>   that I may keep the commands of my God! (v. 115)

> Streams of tears flow from my eyes,
>   for your law is not obeyed. (v. 136)

> My zeal wears me out,
>   for my enemies ignore your words. (v. 139)

> I look on the faithless with loathing,
>   for they do not obey your word. (v. 158)

These are far from pleasant emotions. In fact, in many circumstances some of these emotions would be sinful. Yet, here they are responses to sin and wickedness, and they actually reflect something of God's own reaction to evil. We already touched on this point in section 3, where we looked at personal sin and the word of grace.

This psalmist knows the Scriptures so well that he knows how God feels about sin and indeed how God will eventually act against those who are persistently, unrepentantly wicked.

- God will rebuke them. (v. 21)
- God will reject them. (v. 118)
- God will discard them. (v. 119)

And in the psalmist's opinion it is high time that God did so! (v. 126)

Now of course, the Bible has a great deal more to say about God's love for sinners and God's longing for them to repent so that he can forgive and restore them. As a forgiven sinner himself, this psalmist would not deny that. Indeed, he relies on God's love and forgiveness. But the Bible makes it very clear that deep-rooted, persistent human wickedness stirs God's anger and ultimately brings his judgment.

This raises questions about our own reaction to sin and wickedness in the world around us. Should we as Christians express the same emotions as the psalmist in response to evil, or is such language inappropriate? And what underlies our emotions? Are they really rooted in God's values or are they coloured by fear for our own interests, or by our political loyalties and social prejudices?

What about the *target* of our anger, even when we sincerely believe that our anger is directed against sin? It is easy to become one-sided and to overheat on some moral issues while overlooking others.

Tony Campolo is said to have once announced in a large public gathering that during the course of his talk thousands of the poorest people in the world would die of hunger, "and most of you don't give a ****!" he exclaimed. There was a shocked silence; then some people got up and walked out. "The real shame," he went on, "is that some of you are more morally offended by one bad word than by world poverty and hunger." And he was right, of course. Ezekiel was prepared to use foul language to shock his audience with the far worse moral evil of their own social and private lives. The question we have to ask is, "What makes God most angry?" And where can we find an answer to that question? From the Scriptures of course, as the psalmist did. Did you notice that the main reason why he reacts as he does is because people are not obeying God's word?

So what kind of wickedness does the Bible emphasize?

Well, we might answer, an awful lot of it! But there are some clues as to what God hates most. For example, there is the word "abomination." In Hebrew the word means something that fills God with disgust and revulsion, something he simply cannot stomach. If you do a word search on "abomination", you will find that it covers a surprising list of things. While it includes various forms of sexual immorality, it also includes dishonest scales (Prov 11:1; 20:10, 23). That means that cheating in trade and business is on the list. And if we still feel we are out of range of Scripture's moral firing-power, here are some other things that stink in God's nostrils as abominations.

- False witness and slander (Jer 7:9–10; Ezek 22:9; Prov 6:19)
- Lying in general (Prov 6:16–17; 12:22; 26:25–28)
- Neglect of the poor and needy (Ezek 16:49; 18:12; 22:7)
- Contempt for parents (Ezek 22:7)
- Arrogance (Prov 6:16–19)
- Hypocritical worship (Isa 1:13; Prov 21:27; 28:9)

We might also think of the things that the Bible places under God's curse. Yes, these include idolatry, incest, sexual immorality and murder. But the list also includes abusing the disabled, bribery, and "anyone who withholds justice from the foreigner, the fatherless or the widow" (Deut 27:19).

Turn to Romans 1:18–32 where we find Paul's catalogue of human sin. What did you notice about the list mentioned? Again, we find reference to sexual immorality, murder and depravity. But what other sins are listed? What does this passage teach us about God's standard for living? My point is that we need to educate our anger. That is, we need to have an awareness of *all* that the Bible condemns, and be more consistent and more biblically orientated in the things that stir our emotions and draw our protests.

As evangelical Christians we tend to have our moral consciences focused on sexual problems and devote a huge amount of moral (and church) energy to them. There is no doubt that the Bible speaks out clearly on sexual ethics and that we need to stand for biblical truth in that area. However, it grieves me that nothing like the same moral energy or anger tends to be directed towards social and economic wickedness, perhaps because it is less easy to be sure of the cleanness of our own hands. How disturbed are we, how angry do we find ourselves, when we hear of the plight of refugees, asylum seekers, the homeless, the landless, the family-less, the poor and needy, the victims of oppression, injustice and debt? And yet the anger of God against such things is revealed with devastating clarity throughout the Bible. The Bible has far more to say about these matters than it does about sexual ethics.

- On what grounds to you think the emotions and language of the psalmist are appropriate or inappropriate for Christians today?

- What makes you angry as you listen to the news? Is it the abuse of power, injustice, cruelty, inadequate health care, and bad government, or does something else drive your anger? Analyse your response. Could it be that your own selfish interests are being threatened? Is your response coloured by your political preferences and loyalties or by social prejudices? Can your anger stand the test of clear biblical values?

- How is your church involved in supporting particular moral campaigns in society or taking a stand on certain ethical issues within the church itself? What should our attitudes be towards such things? Discuss and evaluate these attitudes in relation to the Bible's "ethical priorities."

- Is it ever right to be angry when preaching? How can we be very careful that it is God's anger, as clearly expressed in Scripture, and not just our own that we are expressing? And if we do express anger, how can we balance it with biblical words of grace and penitence?

2. The Pain Inside (vv. 25, 28, 50, 81–83, 92, 107, 139)

What was all this struggle and distress doing to the psalmist? We have seen his emotions in relation to external wickedness. But he was also suffering opposition, mockery, slander, false accusation, and possibly even physical threat. So how did he cope with all this? What did it feel like?

There are a number of places in Psalm 119 where the psalmist pours out his feelings. As you read the verses below, reflect on how he feels in each case.

> I am laid low in the dust;
> > preserve my life according to your word. (v. 25)
>
> My soul is weary with sorrow;
> > strengthen me according to your word. (v. 28)

> My comfort in my suffering is this:
>> Your promise preserves my life. (v. 50)
>
> My soul faints with longing for your salvation,
>> but I have put my hope in your word.
> My eyes fail, looking for your promise;
>> I say, "When will you comfort me?"
> Though I am like a wineskin in the smoke,
>> I do not forget your decrees. (vv. 81–83)
>
> If your law had not been my delight,
>> I would have perished in my affliction. (v. 92)
>
> I have suffered much;
>> preserve my life, LORD, according to your word. (v. 107)
>
> My zeal wears me out,
>> for my enemies ignore your words. (v. 139)

What a list of inner pain and struggle! If this person had lived today, he would have been recommended for counselling and a strong dose of pastoral care. The symptoms described include depression, dryness, fainting with exhaustion, extreme weakness and general suffering. It is likely that your church or study group will include some who have experienced very similar feelings. The comfort is that the Bible includes such expressions of pain, allows them to be voiced in the presence of God, and points us in the direction of healing – namely to God himself, his word, his promise and his life-giving strength.

It is worth noting one more thing as we finish. These words of suffering, struggle, weakness and depression come from the lips of one who is a faithful believer. Here is somebody who is sincerely trusting God and doing their absolute utmost to live in obedience to God. And yet this testimony is not one of abundant blessings, or of spectacular outpourings of wealth, or of instant healing.

Reflection and Response

What do you understand by the "prosperity gospel"? Why is it such an attractive teaching? This psalm exposes it as a fraud and a deception. Discuss the dangers of such teaching.[1]

You may find the following helpful to stimulate group discussion:

> "Prosperity" teaching distorts the Bible's teaching and appeals to our natural selfishness and greed. It causes immense spiritual damage. While the Bible certainly gives examples of people whom God blessed with material abundance, it also provides many examples of people who suffered greatly, not because of a lack of faith but because of their determined faith and obedience to God. The Bible is also full of warnings that it is possible to be exceedingly wealthy not as a result of God's blessing but from the profits of oppression and wickedness.

Further Study

Read 2 Corinthians 11:17–18, 21b–30.

Reflect on what Paul suffered for the gospel. How did he respond and what lessons can you draw from this for your own Christian life?

---

1. For further reading see Andrew Perriman (ed.), *Faith, Health and Prosperity* (Carlisle: Paternoster, 2003) and Femi Adeleye, *Preachers of a Different Gospel* (Carlisle: Hippo, 2011).

10

Pressing On

> **AIM: To recommit ourselves to the balance of trust and perseverance**

Focus on the Theme

In our last two studies we tried to understand the circumstances that made the psalmist's life so tough, and we listened to the way he expresses his emotions in response to the evil in the world outside and the pain inside his own heart. But what did the psalmist actually do about all this? The answer is twofold. On the one hand, he cried out desperately to God for help; on the other, he gritted his teeth and carried on. He pleads upwards and he presses onwards.

Read: Psalm 119:145–160

Key verse: Psalm 119:75

Outline

1. Crying out to God (vv. 81–88, 145–148, 150–151, 153–156)
   a. Because God is as near as his troubles are (vv. 145–146)
   b. Because God is a great place to hide (v. 114)
   c. Because God is the God of the exodus (vv. 153–156)
2. Being determined to press on (vv. 28, 32, 67, 71, 75, 81, 83)
3. Conclusion

The psalmist is not the only biblical figure who struggled. So did others like Job and Jeremiah. Even the apostle Paul spoke of being hard pressed, perplexed, persecuted, and struck down. If you read his words in 2 Corinthians 4:7–18, you will see that his response to this suffering has a lot in common with that of the psalmist, although Paul writes in the New Testament era, and so can base his response on what God has done in Christ, whereas the psalmist looked back to the exodus.

1. Crying Out to God (vv. 81–88, 114, 145–146, 150–151, 153–156)

Verses 81–88 are a cry of endurance, a cry born of a desperate, seemingly endless, waiting for God. It is one long drawn out question, "How long must your servant wait?"(v. 84) "I waited patiently for the LORD" says Psalm 40 – but sometimes the psalmist is not so patient: "Lord, when will you hear? When will you answer? When will you do something?"

Many of us know that place and those prayers all too well. We can identify with the psalmist's words below:

> I call with all my heart; answer me, LORD,
> and I will obey your decrees.
> I call out to you; save me
> and I will keep your statutes.
> I rise before dawn and cry for help;
> I have put my hope in your word.
> My eyes stay open through the watches of the night,
> that I may meditate on your promises. (vv. 145–148)

Sleepless nights and early rising testify to the psalmist's anxiety and his deep longing for God to hear his cries. But why does he persist in his confident hope that God will eventually answer and act? Three reasons stand out: because God is near, because God is a shelter and because God is the God of the exodus.

a. Because God is as near as his troubles are (145–146, 150–151)

In fact, God is even nearer than the psalmist's troubles. The psalmist brings this out through a wonderful play on words in these verses:

> Those who devise wicked schemes are near,
> but they are far from your law.

> Yet you are near, LORD,
>> and all your commands are true. (vv. 150–151)

The wicked, who are causing such trouble, seem very near to the psalmist, but they are far from God; whereas God, who seems to be far away from the psalmist (vv. 145–146), is actually near to him.

The nearness of God is a great biblical promise. It is worth remembering when our troubles are bearing down on us. God is nearer than any threat. This promise can be illustrated with an example from a football match I watched on television: an attacker was bearing down on the goalkeeper, and a goal seemed certain. Then suddenly, out of nowhere, another player appeared and robbed the attacker of the ball. At the moment of greatest danger, the unseen defender was even nearer than the striker.

- What other Bible texts speak about the nearness of God?

---

b. Because God is a great place to hide (v. 114)

> You are my refuge and my shield;
>> I have put my hope in your word. (v. 114)

In a storm, you need a shelter. If you are being chased, you need a hiding place. In a bombing raid, you need a bunker. When you were a child you hid under the blankets or ran to your mother's arms. The psalmist loves to picture God as a place to hide. We have a deep need to be safe and secure, and God is the ultimate provider of that security. There are times when we feel so exposed and under attack that running "into God" as the place of shelter and protection is enormously reassuring.

> The name of the LORD is a fortified tower;
>> The righteous run to it and are safe. (Prov 18:10)

When I was principal of All Nations Christian College, there were often times when as a community we were conscious of spiritual attack by the forces of the evil one. As a college dedicated to training people for cross-cultural mission to advance the kingdom of God, this was not at all unexpected. That did not make it any less unpleasant and sometimes almost overwhelming. I remember one occasion when my senior staff team felt there was a particular focus of satanic attack upon myself as principal. We spent time in urgent prayer together. One of my staff prayed a prayer I cannot forget and often re-claim. "Lord," she prayed, "please hide Chris under your wings so that the devil won't even know where to find him." I felt safe after that!

- Which Bible stories illustrate God's nearness at times of great trouble or danger?

---

c. Because God is the God of the exodus (vv. 153–156)

> Look upon my suffering and deliver me;
>   for I have not forgotten your law.
> Defend my cause and redeem me;
>   preserve my life according to your promise.
> Salvation is far from the wicked,
>   for they do not seek out your decrees.
> Your compassion is great, LORD;
>   preserve my life according to your laws. (vv. 153–156)

Where did the psalmist get all this understanding of God from? He has told us again and again that it came from the Torah. He knows about God because he knows the story of the exodus. Of course, the psalmist wasn't personally present at the exodus. But he knew the story, and that story gave him good grounds for faith and hope. It showed that the God Israel worshipped was not blind. No matter how much the wicked seemed to prosper while the righteous suffered, it would not always stay that way. God sees and knows. God cares and acts. God will ultimately defend and redeem his people – including this faithful, praying believer.

So the psalmist asks God to do for him what he originally did for his ancestors, and for the same reasons. The God who saved them is my God too, he reminds himself, so I will call out to him confident that he will hear. He will save and defend me.

Like the psalmist, you should feel free to cry out to God in your troubles. But make sure you know the God you are crying out to. Make sure it is this God, the biblical God; the God you know through your deep immersion in his word.

- Compare the language of the psalm with the story of the exodus as recorded in Exodus 2–6. Notice in particular Exodus 2:23–25; 3:7–9; 6:2–8.

2. Being Determined to Press On (vv. 28, 32, 67, 71, 75, 81, 83)

The psalmist is determined that, no matter what happens, however great the opposition and whatever the cost, he will go on obeying, trusting, serving and loving God. There will be no giving up. He is exercising willpower again as he affirms his stubborn determination to see it through even in the toughest times.

Is this a contradiction? Is it wrong to ask God for help and yet talk about your own efforts and determination? Are we confusing grace and works if we say, "God, you've got to help me, and I cry out to you," and then say "God, I'm determined to keep going, to persevere and struggle through this tough patch"? It cannot be, for both ideas are fully expressed in this one psalm without any sense of conflict between them.

Look at the contrasts in verses 81 and 83. The first half of each verse speaks of the psalmist's longing and exhaustion and cry to God, and the second half speaks of his determination: "I have put my hope in your word"; "I do not forget your decrees." Hope and obedience are to be worked at. God doesn't do them for us; we have to decide to exercise them ourselves. So the psalmist says he will press on. In fact, he will do so with enthusiasm. Look at verses 28 and 32. In verse 28 we hear the cry,

> My soul is weary with sorrow;
> strengthen me according to your word.

But in verse 32 he gathers that strength and says

> I run in the path of your commands,
> for you have broadened my understanding.

The second part of verse 32 is translated as "set my heart free" in earlier NIV versions. So here is somebody who is not just going to crawl determinedly forward in the dust. He's going to get up and run in the path of obedience and the joy of spiritual freedom.

The psalmist also reflects on the fact that some of the struggles that God has allowed him to go through have had a positive effect. Read verses 67, 71 and 75.

> Before I was afflicted I went astray,
> but now I obey your word. (v. 67)

> It was good for me to be afflicted
> so that I might learn your decrees. (v. 71)

> I know, LORD, that your laws are righteous,
> and that in faithfulness you have afflicted me. (v. 75)

When God allows affliction, he does not stop being faithful to us or to himself. This is never an easy lesson to learn. No affliction ever seems a good thing at the time. But just as the irritation caused by a grain of sand produces a pearl in an oyster, so the struggles God allows us to go through can produce good fruit if we choose to persevere in them with God.

We need to hold on to this balance between full confidence in God on the one hand, and courageous perseverance on the other. There are plenty of biblical examples of both that we can learn from.

- What benefit has affliction (suffering) brought? Does this mean that the affliction (suffering) itself was good?

- Read Daniel 3 and Job 1:6–22. How do the people in these stories respond to affliction?

---

3. Conclusion

There are times when we cry:

> Lord, I call out to you again. Lord, I long for you to act. I am desperate for you to sort out this problem, or to put right this mess. Lord, I need you urgently and I know that only you can deal with an issue as big as this one. You are my only hope.

And yet at the same time we say to him:

> But Lord, I am still here waiting in patience. And I want you to know that no matter what you do, and no matter what you don't

do, I'll still be here. You're stuck with me. I'm not going anywhere else. I am your servant; I love you; I trust you. And I'm going to battle on serving you no matter what other people, or Satan, or even you, throw at me. I'm in this for the long haul, for a long obedience in one direction only. For frankly I don't know where else I would go, or what else I would do if I ever gave up on this determination to love and to serve you, the only living God.

This is the voice that we hear from our psalmist. It is also the voice that we hear in the Garden of Gethsemane. There we see the agonizing struggle going on in the Son of God himself. Jesus the man cries out to God in desperate fear of what the next few hours will bring: "My Father, if it is possible, may this cup be taken from me" (Matt 26:39). But immediately he recovers the habit of his whole lifetime and bends his own will to his Father's: "Yet not as I will, but as you will." And in that determination to do what he had come to do, he got up from his knees and walked forward to his arrest, trial, flogging and crucifixion. No one shows us more clearly what utter dependence on God means than Jesus. And no one more clearly models utter determination to press on and do God's will against all the forces of evil drawn up against him.

- Does what the New Testament has to say about struggle and suffering reflect the same faith and determination as Psalm 119? Read and discuss the following passages, noticing the balance of reliance on God and persevering patience and effort. 2 Corinthians 1:3–11; 11:23–30; 12:7–10; Hebrews 12:1–12.

Further Study

Read Nehemiah 2:1–5. You might also want to read Nehemiah 1 to get the context.

Is Nehemiah using the same double strategy as the psalmist? What can this teach us about our own attitude towards struggles and hardships?

Read 2 Corinthians 4:7–18.

Meditate on Paul's response to hardship.

Reflection and Response

If you are meeting with a group, spend time exercising both parts of this double response on behalf of each other. Put each other's needs before God, crying to him to hear and answer as you put your hope and trust in him. Then encourage one another in the daily task of pressing on in faith and obedience.

Read Psalm 40 aloud and make it your own confession.

If you are a preacher, how could you use some of the verses of this psalm to encourage your people to cry out to God when troubles arise, and yet at the same time challenge them to press on and persevere by faith? What biblical examples could you use to make the point come to life?

Section 5

Personal Renewal and the Word of Life

Psalm 119:153–160

Personal Renewal and the Word of Life

Introduction to Section 5

"I shouldn't be here." These are the words spoken directly to the television camera by ordinary people who are enjoying a game of tennis or a family meal or some other everyday activity. The point they are making is that without the life-saving cancer treatment they had received, they would be dead by now. They shouldn't be here, but they are, because the treatment has given them a new and unexpected lease of life. The advertisement ends with a moving appeal to give the gift of life to others through supporting cancer research.

Life. We cling to it, and at times we feel desperately in need of having our lives refreshed and renewed, protected or prolonged. That is certainly the mood of the psalmist.

When I started reading Psalm 119 in depth, I was struck by how frequently this theme comes up. There are 22 sections in the psalm, and in 11 of these, and no less than 14 times in total, the psalmist prays, "Renew my life." Sometimes this is translated, "restore my life," "give me life," "preserve my life," or "let me live." In the majority of cases, these are different ways of rendering a single dramatic exclamation in Hebrew: *Hayyeni!*" Literally it means, "Cause me to live!" or "Make me live!" "'Life' me!" It is a prayer that grows more intense and is repeated more often towards the end of the psalm, and indeed is almost the final prayer, in the last verse but one.

Pause and read the following verses. Read them aloud if possible, one after another, to feel their combined effect and the strength of feeling that goes into this appeal.

> Be good to your servant while I live,
>   that I may obey your word. (v. 17)

> I am laid low in the dust;
>   preserve my life according to your word. (v. 25)

> Turn my eyes away from worthless things;
>   preserve my life according to your word. (v. 37)

How I long for your precepts!
> In your righteousness preserve my life. (v. 40)

My comfort in my suffering is this:
> Your promise preserves my life. (v. 50)

Let your compassion come to me that I may live,
> for your law is my delight. (v. 77)

I have suffered much;
> preserve my life, LORD, according to your word. (v. 107)

Sustain me, my God, according to your promise, and I will live;
> do not let my hopes be dashed. (v. 116)

Your statutes are always righteous;
> give me understanding that I may live. (v. 144)

Hear my voice in accordance with your love;
> preserve my life, LORD, according to your laws. (v. 149)

Defend my cause and redeem me;
> preserve my life according to your promise. (v. 154)

Your compassion, LORD, is great;
> preserve my life according to your laws. (v. 156)

See how I love your precepts;
> preserve my life, LORD, in accordance with your love. (v. 159)

Let me live that I may praise you,
> and may your laws sustain me. (v. 175)

Did you notice, first, how some situation of threat or difficulty is often referred to – something that is "anti-life"? In the psalmist's experience, depression, exhaustion, temptation, hostility and suffering, all make him "die a little." So in chapter 11 we will think about those *threats to life*.

Second, notice that when the psalmist asks God to renew his life, he often makes his appeal on the basis of some fact about God: either God's character (his righteousness, or compassion, or love) or God's word (his law and his promises). We shall think about those *sources of life* in chapter 12.

Third, it is worth noticing that sometimes the psalmist "encourages" God to renew his life with a few suggestions as to what will happen if he does! For the psalmist there would be renewed strength, comfort and hope, of course. But for God there would be renewed obedience and amplified praise coming from the renewed life of his servant. This will form our concluding reflection in this amazing psalmist's company.

11

Threats to Life

> **AIM: To identify and recognize things that may be more life-threatening than we think**

Focus on the Theme

In chapter 8 we looked at some of the struggles the psalmist was going through. But now we notice how he singles out several things that particularly threaten the life he believes he should have from God. These things may not be literally fatal, but they are deadening and debilitating. They spoil the enjoyment of life that God wants us to have. In Psalm 119, the writer mentions three particular things that he sees as threats to life in this sense, namely *depression, selfishness* and *hostility*.

Read: Psalm 119:25–40

Key verse: Psalm 119:37

Outline

1. The threat of depression and exhaustion (vv. 25, 28)
2. The threat of selfish obsession with worthless things (vv. 36–37)
3. The threat of suffering and hostility (vv. 50, 107, 154)

Many things in life are deadly. That is, they are anti-life, they spoil life, they suck the life out of you. Of course, the great original anti-life is sin, as we have known since the garden of Eden. There God warned Adam and Eve that if they ate the fruit of the tree he had told them not to eat, they would "certainly die" (Gen 2:17). When they disobeyed him, they were told that "dust you are and to dust you will return" (Gen 3:19). Paul draws on this story when he says that through sin, death entered human life and history. So sin is the ultimate source of death. But that does not mean that everything that threatens our enjoyment of life is a result of our own sin. Sometimes it is just the fact that we live in a fallen, sinful, death-ridden world. Although we are alive in this world, we live in the midst of death, threatened and invaded by it and by its precursors, the things that rob us of life in the abundance that God intended for us.

I wrote this chapter while meeting with a group of mission personnel in a tough part of Africa. One of them told me about her struggles. Her commitment to serving in Chad for seventeen years had taken a toll on her health, and she endured bouts of chronic fatigue. She loved the Lord and she loved his word. She loved her work too, but there was too much of it. She was overloaded with work and with trying to meet the expectations of others. Her exhaustion bred a dusty dryness of spirit, depression and guilt, and fear of relapsing into debilitating illness. Together we prayed for God to renew and restore her life. The prayer of this psalmist is exactly the same as her longing.

1. The Threat of Depression and Exhaustion (vv. 25, 28)

> I am laid low in the dust;
>   preserve my life according to your word. (v. 25)
>
> My soul is weary with sorrow;
>   strengthen me according to your word. (v. 28)

The psalmist speaks of being "laid low in the dust," of being utterly exhausted and worn out. "Dust" is, of course, an echo of the dust of death in Genesis 3:19. We see it used in the same way by the teacher in Ecclesiastes, who ends his poetic meditation on death by speaking of the dust to which we all return (Eccl 12:7). But the writer of Psalm 119 feels he is eating the dust already. Life is dried and shrivelled. This is the way people feel when they are deeply depressed.

Depression can, of course, be a relatively mild thing. When life isn't going well for some reason, you may feel miserable about everything or about something specific. But the psalmist is probably talking about more than feeling depressed for a few days. We know that severe depression can be a terrible, frightening experience. It may be caused by prolonged stress, emotional pressures, unresolved traumas, broken relationships, bereavement, and other sometimes inexplicable factors, and it can also have a physiological dimension. It can constitute a serious clinical illness. Some of us may have been there, and those of us who have family members or friends who suffer from serious depression know something of how brutal it can be.

One of the things I have frequently heard from those who suffer from periodic bouts of depression is exactly what this psalmist seems to say: Life doesn't seem worth living any more. All the point has gone out of it. There is no joy or hope in anything – not even in the simplest of pleasures that are part of the fabric of everyday life. Favourite food loses its flavour. Everything seems under a cloud of futility. Depression, in that sense, is life-destroying. You don't have to be physically dead to feel as if you might as well be. Death has impinged on life.

And believers are not immune to depression. Sometimes even the godliest, most committed people, filled with the Spirit of God, living lives of Christlikeness and service to God, are like this psalmist in being "laid low in the dust." It's not because they haven't got faith, or that they don't pray enough, any more than you could say this about the psalmist.

We are not told whether the psalmist goes through such torment because of sickness, or sin, or exhaustion, or opposition. Whatever it is, did you notice the symptoms? Loss of any sense of time and purpose, inner pain, loss of appetite, loss of weight, loss of friends, loss of sleep . . .

It is out of such depths that the cry comes, *"Lord, give me back my life!"*

- If you need to talk to someone about the issues that have been raised here, you could turn to a close friend or a Christian counsellor. Alternatively, read Psalm 102:1–11 and try to enter into the life-sucking experience of the psalmist. The heading of that psalm describes it as the "prayer of an afflicted person who has grown weak and pours out a lament before the LORD." Try to capture the psalmist's feelings by writing out that passage in your own paraphrase.

- If you preach on such texts as these, be aware that there may well be people listening who are suffering from depression – whether they have told you so or not (many sufferers from depression are quite good at concealing it). Be pastorally careful and sensitive in what you say.

2. The Threat of Selfish Obsession with Worthless Things (vv. 36–37)

An obsession with worthless things is the second life-threatening, death-injecting thing that the psalmist brings to God asking for deliverance. He recognizes that temptation usually starts with what we see, and then start to covet, and so in the verses that follow he asks God to turn his eyes away from temptations and to keep his heart (or his mind, in Hebrew terms) focused on God.

> Turn my heart toward your statutes
>   and not toward selfish gain.
> Turn my eyes away from worthless things;
>   preserve my life according to your word. (vv. 36–37)

The psalmist is wise enough to discern that when you focus on your own desires, obsessed by greed and covetousness and material gain, it actually delivers the opposite effect. Instead of gaining anything, you lose everything. Instead of getting a better life, you risk losing the life you had.

Jesus warned "where your treasure is, there your heart will be also" (Matt 6:21) and carried on to say, "What good will it be for someone to gain the whole world, yet forfeit their soul? Or what can anyone give in exchange for their soul?" (Matt 16:26). The psalmist, aware at least in some measure of this danger, prays that God will keep him from becoming obsessed with things that will waste his life, things that promise life but deliver death.

"Selfish gain" and "worthless things" cover a lot of possibilities. Certainly one of them, and one of the most dangerous, is material wealth. Jesus gave us one of his sharpest warnings about that: "Watch out! Be on your guard against all kinds of greed; life does not consist in an abundance of possessions" (Luke 12:15).

Then there was Jesus's encounter with the rich young man who actually asked Jesus, like this psalmist, for his recipe for eternal life. The man wanted to be among those who would stand among the redeemed and righteous people of God on the last day, inheriting the life of the age to come, the new life of the kingdom of God that Jesus was talking about. And Jesus told him. Among other things, Jesus put his finger on the thing in the young man's life that was actually standing in the way of inheriting real life. This thing that was death-dealing. It was his obsession with his personal wealth and his refusal to let it go and follow Jesus. The tragedy of the story is that, having been pointed to the way of life, the rich young man turned around and walked away sad, returning to the way of death (Matt 19:16–22). He would not allow Jesus to do what this psalmist prays for: to turn his heart away from selfish gain and worthless things, in order to find renewal of life according to the word of the Lord.

- In what ways are "worthless things" the enemy of life and in what ways is "selfish gain" contrary to God's statutes?

- Are there things in your life that could be described as "worthless things" or "selfish gain"? Be careful to distinguish them from ordinary pleasures and relaxations that God blesses us with and invites us to enjoy. What will it mean for you to recognize the threat such things pose to God's purpose for your life?

3. The Threat of Suffering and Hostility (vv. 50, 107, 154)

The third life-threatening set of circumstances, that we hear about when the psalmist prays for God to preserve or renew his life, is suffering and especially (I think) suffering caused by the hostility, opposition or criticism of others.

> My comfort in my suffering is this:
> Your promise preserves my life. (v. 50)

> I have suffered much;
> preserve my life, LORD, according to your word. (v. 107)

> Defend my cause and redeem me;
> preserve my life according to your promise. (v. 154)

It is the third verse that gives the clue. "Redeem me" does not mean that the psalmist is asking for personal forgiveness for his own sin. No, he is asking for deliverance from the attacks of others. He needs rescue. He needs somebody to take his side and stand up for him. This suggests that the suffering in verses 50 and 107 was caused by something similar to the issues we observed in chapter 8. It was being caused by the sustained hostility and opposition this person was enduring in whatever public role he was trying to fulfil. And the psalmist cries out asking God not only to comfort him, defend him and redeem him but also to preserve his life. The guy is being hounded to death. Prolonged hostility is crushing the life out of him.

It can be a deathly thing to live with the internalized pain of depression. It can also be deathly to live with the external pain of constant criticism, opposition and hostility. Many Christians live with opposition and even persecution from non-Christian family, or colleagues, or political authorities. Even within the Christian church itself, sadly, there are people who ought to know better who go around making life a misery for their pastors and leaders. It can be soul-destroying, life-crushing and death-dealing.

You may have been there, and if so you know something of the dark numbness that comes when constant criticism squeezes the life and joy out of you. If that's the case, Psalms 55 and 56 were written with you in mind. There are times when you probably long, like the psalmist, for the wings of a dove, to be able to fly away and leave it all behind (Ps 55:6–8). And there are other times when you hold on grimly to the great affirmation of Psalm 56:11.

> In God I trust and am not afraid.
> What can man do to me?

Or it could be that you are among those who deal out the criticism relentlessly. Can I urge you to be cautious, no matter how justified you and your friends may feel your complaints and opposition to be? Be careful. Maybe you do it out of what you think are the best of motives. But make sure you do it (if you have to) also as before the Lord, and with his spirit of grace and compassion. If you have to "speak the truth in love" (another sadly abused verse), make sure that what you say is constructive, not destructive; life-giving not life-sapping. Christian leaders can be criticized to death. Don't be among the assassins.

- Pray, with the psalmist, "Lord, renew my life according to your word." Recognize that such renewal may need to come along with repentance and some fresh resolution and exercise of the will (see ch. 6).

- Do you experience opposition to your preaching? Think carefully about what the reasons may be. Is it because you are truly explaining and applying the word of God and people don't like it? Or is it because you are constantly inflicting your own opinions and pet themes on them? If it is the first, you will need to pray some of the verses of this psalm.

Further Study

Read 2 Corinthians 4:11–12.

What are some of the ways in which we can see death "at work in us" and in the world around us? How are we to respond to this dying and decaying world?

Do you have a favourite Bible passage to turn to in trouble and conflict? There are some wonderful words of encouragement in the Bible. Turn to Isaiah 55:6–13 and let this inspire words of praise and thankfulness to our God, despite your present circumstances or difficulties.

Reflection and Response

We live in a world where our lives are constantly invaded by things that reek of death – emotional, spiritual and psychological death – even when they are not a threat to our physical lives. Like the psalmist, we need to identify such things, name them and shame them, and claim the power of the life-giving God over them.

What could be eating away at your life? It could be unconfessed sin (see Ps 32). Or it could be stubbornness, pride, or self-pity. It could be disobedience or an ungodly relationship. Whatever it is, recognize its life-threatening nature, and make the psalmist's prayer your own: "Lord, renew my life, restore my life, give my life back and let me live it fully for you."

12

Sources of Life

> **AIM: To remind ourselves of the true meaning and source of renewal**

Focus on the Theme

When the psalmist needed an answer to the problem of sin, he knew where (and where alone) to look – to God himself (see ch. 7). In the same way, when he was conscious of things that threatened his life in some way (see ch. 11), he knew where the only source of true life is to be found – in God. And so in all the verses where he asks for life, he bases his request on God's character and God's word. It is the same for us. We too can turn to God for his gift of renewed life because of who God is and because of what God has said.

Read: Psalm 119:169–176

Key verse: Psalm 119:175

Outline

1. The character of God (vv. 40, 77, 159)
   a. God's righteousness (v. 40)
   b. God's compassion (v. 77)
   c. God's love (v. 159)
2. The words of God (vv. 25, 37, 50, 107, 116, 149, 154, 156)
   a. "Your word" (vv. 25, 37, 107)
   b. "Your promise" (vv. 50, 116, 154)

c. "Your laws" (vv. 149, 156)
3. Renewal and its effects (vv. 17, 175)
   a. Obedience
   b. Praise
   c. Renewal

I'm Martin, I'm here, and I'm alive," he said, at the start of a sharing time during the conference in Africa that I mentioned in the last chapter. Martin's testimony was that, though it was obvious he was alive, standing there in front of us, it was not something he or we should take for granted. God had delivered him from potentially fatal accidental electrocution, and later from an arson attack. And his emotional life, which had broken down about a year earlier through a combination of personal factors and the stresses of life in Christian mission, had been restored by God's grace. God had given him his life back. So we praised God with him: for his faithfulness, his gentleness, for the angels of mercy he sends in times of need, and above all for his word – his life-giving word.

1. The Character of God (vv. 40, 77, 159)

The psalmist knew that God's character was the reason he could confidently appeal to him for life. So in this psalm he focuses on three aspects of God's character, namely his righteousness, his compassion and his love.

a. God's righteousness (v. 40)

> How I long for your precepts!
>   In your righteousness preserve my life. (v. 40)

Verse 40 may come as a surprise because we are inclined to think of God's righteousness in terms of judgment, wrath and punishment. We can never match up to his righteousness, and so we tend to think of it as a measuring rod that will be used as a rod to beat us. Martin Luther tells us that he used to think about it in those terms, and so he was very puzzled by Paul's statement that righteousness from God is revealed in the gospel (Rom 1:17). In the law, yes, but how in the gospel?

Although it is true that God's judgment of sinners is an outworking of his righteous character, in the Old Testament the righteousness of God is more often associated with his salvation than with his wrath. If you find this hard to believe, get a concordance and look up all the occurrences of the words "righteous" or "righteousness" as applied to God. The LORD (*Yahweh*) is the God who vindicates, delivers, saves and rescues people. That is, he gets them out of a wrong situation and puts them right. And that's what "doing righteousness" means. So, as Isaiah 45:21 says, he is "a righteous God and a Saviour." That does not mean "a righteous God, but nevertheless in spite of that, he sometimes does some saving too." The two phrases are parallel; they basically mean the same thing. The Lord is a righteous God, and *therefore* he is the Saviour of his people out of their sin and slavery.

In the Old Testament the righteousness of God means God in action putting things right. Putting things right involves both identifying and punishing those who are doing wrong, and vindicating and uplifting those who are being wronged – the innocent party in a lawsuit, the oppressed in a situation of injustice. For the latter, it would be like getting their life back. For somebody falsely accused of a capital offence, it would literally be having their life spared.

So now we can make sense of why our psalmist appeals to God's righteousness when he asks God to preserve his life. He is not saying, "Save me God because *I am righteous*, or because I deserve your favour, or can claim your attention because I've earned your blessing." No, he pleads, "save me God, but only because *you are righteous*. You are the God whose righteous acts of salvation and deliverance are part of our national history. Your righteousness is the good news on which I rest my hope of life."

We know, of course, in light of the New Testament, that the saving righteousness of God was ultimately demonstrated on the cross. As Paul explains in Romans, the sacrifice of Christ was simultaneously God's righteous judgment on sin and his saving righteousness for sinners. That is why he can say

> I am not ashamed of the gospel, because it is the power of God that brings salvation to everyone who believes: first to the Jew, then to the Gentile. For in the gospel the righteousness of God is revealed – a righteousness that is by faith from first to last, just as it is written: "the righteous will live by faith." (Rom 1:16–17)

It took Martin Luther some time to understand this truth. But he began to grasp it as he taught a course on the Psalms at Wittenberg University, where he taught for many years before he became the famous Reformer. It was as he was teaching the Psalms that he began to understand that "the righteousness of God" means his saving righteousness. From that perspective, the puzzling text in Romans came to make perfect sense. It was reading the Psalms that led him to his great recovery of the truth of justification by grace through faith.

To understand more of God's righteousness, read and think about the following passages from Psalms:

Psalm 35:24–28

- What do you think is the background to this appeal?
- What will it mean for the psalmist if God acts on his behalf in righteousness?
- What will it mean for those who are attacking him?

Psalm 37:5–10

- This is not so much an appeal as a celebration. What words does the writer link up in poetic parallelism?
- In light of verse 10, is it possible to contrast God's love and God's righteousness and set them off one against the other? Why do we sometimes do that?

Psalm 40:9–10

- The psalmist says he is going to "preach righteousness." What do you think he means by that? In the light of all the texts above, how do you preach about the righteousness of God?

---

b. God's compassion (v. 77)

> Let your compassion come to me that I may live,
>   for your law is my delight. (v. 77)

In English we say "we have given our hearts to the Lord," but in some African languages they say, "We have given our stomachs to the Lord." The stomach for them symbolizes the centre of their being. For the Hebrews, the seat of emotions was even lower down – in the bowels. That's where you really feel stuff, especially pity and sympathy. The Hebrew word translated "compassion" in verse 77 speaks of that deep emotion you feel deep down inside, "in your guts" as we might say. That's where God feels his pity and compassion for us. It is the inner movement of his feelings of tender compassion towards the needy.

As we saw in Section 3, "compassion" is a term found on God's name-badge in the Old Testament. It is of the essence of God's personal identity. It was first heard by Moses in the cleft of the rock when God proclaimed his name to him:

> And he passed in front of Moses, proclaiming, "the LORD, the LORD, the compassionate and gracious God, slow to anger, abounding in love and faithfulness, maintaining love to thousands, and forgiving wickedness, rebellion and sin. Yet he does not leave the guilty unpunished." (Exod 34:6-7)

In chapter 7 we saw how much the compassion and grace of God meant to this psalmist in relation to sin. Here it becomes part of his quest for life. This is the spirituality that nourished our psalmist. He wanted life, so he ran to the compassion of God, encouraging us to do the same.

- Psalm 103 also relates God's compassion to the gift of life in all its fullness. You probably know it well. But read it through slowly now, savouring the life-enriching blessings of verses 1-5, the link with righteousness in verses 6-7, the echo of Exodus 34:6 in verse 8, and the comparison with parental compassion in verse 13.

---

c. God's love (v. 159)

> See how I love your precepts;
> preserve my life, LORD, in accordance with your love. (v. 159)

Two different Hebrew words are used here: both are translated "love" in English and both can be used of either humans or God. *Hesed* ("your love") means covenantal, faithful love, committed loyalty to a relationship. It too is one of the defining characteristics of Yahweh – so much so that Psalm 136 repeats it 26 times, for every single verse includes the refrain "His love endures forever" (literally, "for unto eternity is his *hesed*").

The psalmist wants life, so he appeals to God's love, because love is life-giving. Even in ordinary human relationships we know that. When somebody loves you, life is better! People have literally been loved back to life and health.

Love is what supports and revives people, lifting them out of the depths of sorrow and pain. How many great novels and movies have celebrated this fact? Committed love is the source of all that makes life worth living.

How much more true is it, then, that the love of God is life-giving? Indeed, Psalm 63:3 puts God's love above life itself.

> Because your love is better than life,
>   my lips will glorify you.

God's love is the essence of the gospel. It is the love of God that brings eternal life, "for God so loved the world that he gave his one and only Son, that whoever believes in him shall not perish but have eternal life" (John 3:16).

When our psalmist longs for God to give him life, or to renew and restore, or to preserve his life, he doesn't merely draw God's attention to the awful plight he is in. He doesn't just say "Look at me, God." He says, "Lord, give me life because of who you are. You are the righteous, compassionate, loving God. That is your character. And on that basis I appeal to you to pour your own life into mine. Give me life!"

Where do you go when you know your life needs renewal and refreshment? Where do you go to get a life? Books? Conferences? A Christian holiday resort? Special courses or retreats? The latest spiritual technique?

Have you tried God?

When you do try God, make sure it is the God of the Bible to whom you turn and not some figment of your own imagination, or somebody else's successfully marketed recipe for the good life (spiritually speaking of course). No, seek this God, the Lord God, the living God of Scripture – the God of righteousness, compassion and love.

- Psalm 119 links the renewal of life to God's righteousness, compassion and love. What other characteristics or attributes of God could you add to that list? Try to support your answers with specific Bible passages.

- If you are a preacher, how often do you preach Bible texts that teach these great truths about God himself? We can be tempted to preach mostly on texts that encourage *us* to do things – to repent, or trust, or be more honest, or whatever. But it is when people get to know the deep biblical truths about the righteousness, compassion and love of the living God, that they find comfort and hope – life itself.

---

2. The Words of God (vv. 25, 37, 50, 107, 116, 149, 154, 156)

Of the fourteen verses in which the psalmist asks God to renew his life or let him live,[1] eight link the request to some dimension of the word of God with the phrase, "according to . . ." followed by one of his favourite expressions for the word of God.[2] When the psalmist asks God for life, he asks for it according to God's *word* (three times), God's *promise* (three times) and God's *laws* (twice). We will look at each of these in turn.

a. "Your word" (vv. 25, 37, 107)

Each of the following three verses refers to a different threatening experience, but they all offer a single solution – the word of God.

> I am laid low in the dust;
>   preserve my life according to your word. (v. 25)
>
> Turn my eyes away from worthless things;
>   preserve my life according to your word. (v. 37)
>
> I have suffered much;
>   preserve my life, LORD, according to your word. (v. 107)

When we speak of the word of God, we normally mean the books in the Old Testament and New Testament that we call the Bible. Old Testament believers, of course, only had some portions of the Bible, depending on when they lived. But they loved and revered the Scriptures they had (as this psalmist demonstrates). And they also knew a thing or two about the word of God in a wider and deeper sense.

In particular they associated the word of God with the power of God in creation. We know this from the first chapter of the Bible, of course, where God spoke his word and stuff happened. The psalmists revelled in it.

> By the word of the LORD the heavens were made,
>   their starry host by the breath of his mouth.
> He gathers the waters of the sea into jars;
>   he puts the deep into storehouses.
> Let all the earth fear the LORD;

---

1. All cited on pp. 103–104 in the introduction to section 5.
2. See page 4 of the Introduction for the eight different Hebrew expressions used in Psalm 119.

> let all the people of the world revere him.
> For he spoke, and it came to be;
> > he commanded, and it stood firm. (Ps 33:6–9)

It is easy for us to become so familiar with biblical teaching on creation that we stop being astonished at the incredible scale of what is affirmed in this beautiful poetry. Everything in the universe, from the equations that govern galaxies down to the stupendous complexity of the information in the DNA in every cell of your body – it was the word of God that brought it into existence and sustains it every day. The stars in the universe? God's breath. The oceans? God's got them in a jam jar. The whole planet Earth? It's only here because God commanded it.

If, then, the word of God is the source of all life anywhere in the universe, no wonder the psalmist figures it must be the best place to go if it's life you need. Go to the living God. Get life from his living word. As Charles Wesley wrote in his hymn, "O for a thousand tongues":

> He speaks, and, listening to his voice,
> > new life the dead receive.

- What is it about the word of God that is life-giving in difficult circumstances?

- Can you or anyone in your group testify to prayers like the psalmist's being answered through the word of God?

- Do you need to renew your confidence, as a preacher, that God's word is life-giving? Pray that God will bring his word to life for you as you study it, so that you can use it to bring life to others.

---

b. "Your promise" (vv. 50, 116, 154)

The verses quoted below all connect the psalmist's desire for life to God's promise. In each case, notice what he wants specifically, which he believes the promises of God will supply.

> My comfort in my suffering is this:
> > Your promise preserves my life. (v. 50)

> Sustain me, my God, according to your promise, and I will live;
>> do not let my hopes be dashed. (v. 116)
>
> Defend my cause and redeem me;
>> preserve my life according to your promise. (v. 154)

Comfort, hope and deliverance are the key words: comfort in suffering, hope to sustain him in times of weakness, rescue from vicious attack. He looks to God's promises in such circumstances. That's where he will find life in the face of such struggles.

- We are familiar with the many great and precious promises we read in the New Testament, but what were the specific promises this Old Testament believer would have known?

---

c. "Your laws" (vv. 149, 156)

We can understand God giving life through his word and his promises, but would we have thought of asking God for life "according to your laws"? Note the word that is put in parallel with "your laws" in each of the verses below.

> Hear my voice in accordance with your love;
>> preserve my life, LORD, according to your laws. (v. 149)
>
> Your compassion, LORD, is great;
>> preserve my life according to your laws. (v. 156)

The reason we may find this puzzling is because we hear echoes, in the back of our minds, of the stern words of the apostle Paul in Romans and Galatians about how the law brings condemnation and death. But it is important to see Paul's writing in the context of the conflict he was involved in theologically with those who had turned the law into a burden. For such people, keeping the law was the defining mark of their membership in God's covenant people, and the law functioned as an exclusion zone for all non-Jews. Paul himself had lived that way as he tells us in Philippians 3:1–6, but now he had found righteousness and salvation through faith in Christ. It was faith, not law that was the primary requirement. But that was also true in the Old Testament! Paul's quarrel was not with the Old Testament as such, but with those who had distorted it into a system that had lost touch with its true heart – relationship with God through faith in his promise and trust in his grace.

We should remember that Psalm 119 and all the others that celebrate God's law (like Pss 1 and 19) are part of the Scriptures that Paul knew and loved. He believed what this psalmist believed, and doubtless would and could have prayed the prayer in the verses above.

Why then does the psalmist ask for life "according to your laws"? What is there in the law that was life-giving? Well, notice again the two words that he associates with God's law: love and compassion. Where did the Israelites learn of the love and compassion of God? From their stories, yes, but also from the laws that God had given them. In many of these laws, the Israelites were commanded to show love and compassion to others, and in that way to imitate God himself. For example, the law commanded them to show compassion (sometimes life-saving compassion) for specific groups like refugee slaves (Deut 23:15–16), poor debtors (Deut 15:7–11; 24:6, 10–13), poor labourers (Deut 24:14–15), the landless and family-less (Deut 14:28–29; 24:19–22), the disabled (Lev 19:14) and foreigners (Exod 23:9; Lev 19:33–34).

Why should Israel behave like this? Because this was "the way of the LORD." Yahweh was the God of compassion, and so he exercised loving care for the needy. The author of Psalm 146:7–9 knew this, and he knew it from laws like those mentioned in the previous paragraph. God provided them as a model for Israelites:

> For the LORD your God is God of gods and Lord of lords, the great God, mighty and awesome, who shows no partiality and accepts no bribes. He defends the cause of the fatherless and the widow, and loves the foreigner residing among you, giving them food and clothing. And you are to love those who are foreigners, for you yourselves were foreigners in Egypt. (Deut 10:17–19)

God told the Israelites that he had given them his law to preserve and enhance their life. Obedience would be good for them and sustain long life in the land of promise. Deuteronomy makes this point repeatedly. So much so, that in appealing to the Israelites to follow God's law when they got into the land, Moses told them that they were being faced with a choice between life and death.

> This day I call the heavens and the earth as witnesses against you that I have set before you life and death, blessings and curses. Now choose life, so that you and your children may live and that you may love the LORD your God, listen to his voice, and hold fast to

him. For the LORD is your life, and he will give you many years in the land he swore to give to your fathers, Abraham, Isaac and Jacob. (Deut 30:19–20)

Now we can see why the psalmist links his desire for life with God's law. He is saying, in effect, "Lord, I want you to restore my life, and I know from your law that that is what you want too. Your law tells me that you are the God who cares for the poor, the needy and the alien. And that is what I am, what I feel like right now. So, Lord, please renew and protect my life, just as you say in your laws."

Again and again we find that this person finds all he needs in the Scriptures. That is where he learns about God, about God's ways and character, about God's words, promises and laws. No wonder then that he appeals to God according to the Scriptures that he knows so well. It is an example we need to follow a lot more than we do. The psalmist prays for renewal of life, and he encourages us to do the same, seeking it from the same source.

- Exodus 34:6–8 echoes like a bell through the Old Testament. Read through each of the following passages where it occurs, noting the context and background in each case, and how much the Old Testament believers relished and relied upon this bedrock truth about their God: Numbers 14:18; Nehemiah 9:17; Psalm 86:15; Psalm 145:8; Joel 2:13; Jonah 4:2.

- Can you think of any New Testament passages where the same truth is expressed, in different words, in the light of the cross?

---

3. Renewal and Its Effects (vv. 17, 175)

Reading again through the list of 14 verses in which the Psalmist prays for renewal of life, we notice that he sometimes adds a word of "motivation" to God to answer his prayer. Something will happen, if only God gives him his life back. Well, for the psalmist it's fairly obvious what those things are. We've looked at them already. He will receive comfort in sorrow, hope to sustain him, strength to keep on keeping on, courage in the face of suffering and hostility. We know about these things. We can identify with the psalmist.

But what's in it for God? What will God get if he answers this person's prayer and gives him a new lease of life, or protects his life from the danger he may be in? Look again at the first and last of the list of prayers for life. Notice the particular resolve the psalmist makes, should the Lord allow him to live.

> Be good to your servant, while I live,
>   that I may obey your word. (v. 17)

> Let me live that I may praise you,
>   and may your laws sustain me. (v. 175)

Two things stand out: obedience and praise. In fact, it is worth noticing that the first time the psalmist asks God for life, it is so that God will have his obedience; the last time he does so (in the penultimate verse of the whole psalm) it is so that God will have all his praise. There is something very healthy about this. It stands out against any self-centred bargaining that is at the core of "prosperity teaching."

a. Obedience

Why should God be good to me and let me live? So that I can get on with doing what he wants to be done. Why should any of us, sinners that we are, be spared to enjoy life at all, except to find our fulfilment of life in loving, serving and obeying our Maker and Redeemer? There is a wonderful dynamic cycle of life within Old Testament faith, which you find running through the Law and the Psalms especially. God's blessing gives us life. As we live, we obey him in response to his grace and blessing. That in turn leads to further blessing, which leads to renewed obedience. It all flows from grace, through gratitude, into obedience, back to blessing and onwards to God's own glory and pleasure.

- Read Deuteronomy 30:19–20, a passage that may well have been in the psalmist's mind. What does it mean in your own daily life (or in the experience of members of the group), to "choose life" and to acknowledge that "the Lord is your life"?

---

b. Praise

Towards the end of this psalm in which we have found so much lament, struggle, suffering and exhaustion, is a longing for life so that God can be praised.

There is a touching pre-resurrection faith at work here. Old Testament believers did not lack a growing awareness that God had power over death and that their relationship with God would not be destroyed by death. But it was life here and now on God's good earth that filled most of their horizon. So the psalmist is saying to God, "Lord, if I die, who is going to be praising you then? My bones? The dust? Not much, I think, so let me live that I may praise you, while I have life and breath!" The same perspective comes in the similar plea for life in Psalm 30:9.

> What is gained if I am silenced,
>   if I go down into the pit?
> Will the dust praise you?
>   Will it proclaim your faithfulness?

Although the final note of the psalm is one of praise, the final verse of the psalm shows that it does not mean happy-clappy joyfulness. This person still feels like a lost sheep, in need of being found again and brought back by and to God.

It is good to remind ourselves again at this point that praise in the Bible is more than joyfulness – indeed it can function in the apparent absence of joy. It is not something we do when we have no troubles, or as a way of escaping from our troubles; we do it in the midst of them. One of the things I get annoyed about in some worship times is when the leader invites us to "Leave all the things that have been on our minds and bothering us before we came to church. Leave them behind and let's just come into God's presence and praise the Lord." But what does that achieve? All it means is that you think you've been praising God, and then you go back to your troubles. They are waiting for you at the door of the church; you pick them up as you go out, but you haven't brought them into the presence of God. The psalmists don't do that. They bring everything before God, and sometimes they throw them down in front of him and challenge him to do something and ask how long they have to wait. And that too is praise. For it is acknowledging the reality and the presence and power of God and bringing *all of life* before him.

So this psalmist is not saying, "Lord, restore my life and we'll all live happily ever after." Life is not a fairy story. No, he says, "Lord, restore my life and I will praise you with my whole being, even when I feel like a lost sheep, even when life is tough, even when I wonder where you are and when you will act."

c. Renewal

"Renewal" is an over-used word today that sometimes gets twisted away from its biblical roots and meaning. In some circles it seems to be a kind of spiritual narcissism. "Look how blessed and renewed I am! You can have the same renewal we've been having, if you just do what we do." People want renewal and blessing, but they are not perhaps willing to live lives of obedience and praise, even in the midst of their struggle – as this psalmist did. Yet surely, renewal without obedience is a fake. And renewal without sincere praise to God in the whole of life is nothing but self-focused idolatry.

- If we ask God for a renewed life, what impact should it have on us, and what does that mean for you in practice when you finish this Bible study and go back to "life in the real world"?

Further Study

Read Isaiah 40:28–31.

We are told that if we "hope in the LORD" our strength will be renewed. What does it mean to hope in the Lord? How should this affect the way we view struggles and difficulties?

Reflection and Response

Make a list for yourself, or as a group, of promises from the Old Testament that bring comfort, hope and protection from God into your life. Here are a few to get you started:

- Joshua 1:5
- Psalm 23
- Isaiah 43:1–2
- Jeremiah 29:11
- Daniel 3:16–18

Add more, and claim their life-giving power for your particular needs.

Conclusion

We have walked a long way in the company of the person who composed this marvellous psalm.

- We have been impressed with his deep commitment to the word of God and its eternal moral truth, and challenged by the strength and passion of such a worldview.
- We have witnessed his longing to be guided by God and to walk in God's way, finding light and learning through God's word.
- We have identified with his acute awareness of sin and all the horrendous damage it does in human life, and shared his longing to avoid it and find in God our only answer through his forgiving grace.
- We have noted some of the struggles he was going through, externally and internally, and heard his laments and protests, recognizing that these are words that not only speak to us (as God's word), but also often speak for us.
- And we have heard his recurrent longing for life itself – the renewed, restored, abundant life that only God can give – because of who God is and the things God has said.

It would be good to finish by reading the final section of this great poem slowly and aloud. For it is here that so many of the psalm's themes surface again.

> May my cry come before you, LORD;
>   give me understanding according to your word.
> May my supplication come before you;
>   deliver me according to your promise.
> May my lips overflow with praise,
>   for you teach me your decrees.
> May my tongue sing of your word,
>   for all your commands are righteous.
> May your hand be ready to help me,
>   for I have chosen your precepts.
> I long for your salvation, LORD,
>   and your law gives me delight.

> Let me live that I may praise you,
>> and may your laws sustain me.
> I have strayed like a lost sheep.
>> Seek your servant,
>> for I have not forgotten your commands. (vv. 169–176)

And as we reflect on the psalmist's final prayer in the last verse, isn't it a great comfort to know that at the end of the day, as at the end of this psalm, it is the responsibility of the shepherd to find the lost sheep, not the responsibility of the sheep to find the shepherd?

May the Lord himself seek and find each one of us, as we seek him, his word and his will for our lives.

Langham
PARTNERSHIP

Langham Literature and its imprints are a ministry of Langham Partnership.

Langham Partnership is a global fellowship working in pursuit of the vision God entrusted to its founder John Stott –

> *to facilitate the growth of the church in maturity and Christ-likeness through raising the standards of biblical preaching and teaching.*

Our vision is to see churches in the Majority World equipped for mission and growing to maturity in Christ through the ministry of pastors and leaders who believe, teach and live by the word of God.

Our mission is to strengthen the ministry of the word of God through:
- nurturing national movements for biblical preaching
- fostering the creation and distribution of evangelical literature
- enhancing evangelical theological education

especially in countries where churches are under-resourced.

Our ministry

Langham Preaching partners with national leaders to nurture indigenous biblical preaching movements for pastors and lay preachers all around the world. With the support of a team of trainers from many countries, a multi-level programme of seminars provides practical training, and is followed by a programme for training local facilitators. Local preachers' groups and national and regional networks ensure continuity and ongoing development, seeking to build vigorous movements committed to Bible exposition.

Langham Literature provides Majority World preachers, scholars and seminary libraries with evangelical books and electronic resources through publishing and distribution, grants and discounts. The programme also fosters the creation of indigenous evangelical books in many languages, through writer's grants, strengthening local evangelical publishing houses, and investment in major regional literature projects, such as one volume Bible commentaries like *The Africa Bible Commentary* and *The South Asia Bible Commentary*.

Langham Scholars provides financial support for evangelical doctoral students from the Majority World so that, when they return home, they may train pastors and other Christian leaders with sound, biblical and theological teaching. This programme equips those who equip others. Langham Scholars also works in partnership with Majority World seminaries in strengthening evangelical theological education. A growing number of Langham Scholars study in high quality doctoral programmes in the Majority World itself. As well as teaching the next generation of pastors, graduated Langham Scholars exercise significant influence through their writing and leadership.

To learn more about Langham Partnership and the work we do visit **langham.org**

Lightning Source UK Ltd.
Milton Keynes UK
UKHW020823010221
378045UK00001B/45